Willis Lord

The Blessed Hope

Or, the glorious coming of the Lord

Willis Lord

The Blessed Hope
Or, the glorious coming of the Lord

ISBN/EAN: 9783337101848

Printed in Europe, USA, Canada, Australia, Japan

Cover: Foto ©Lupo / pixelio.de

More available books at **www.hansebooks.com**

THE BLESSED HOPE:

OR,

THE GLORIOUS COMING

OF THE LORD.

"Every eye shall see Him."—REVELATION 1: 7.

BY

WILLIS LORD, D. D.

CHICAGO:

W. G. HOLMES, 77 MADISON STREET,
1877.

A. J. GOFF & CO., PRINTERS, CHICAGO.

Contents

Prayer.

Most Holy Spirit of God! Guide Thou the writer and the readers of this little book into the knowledge of Him, of whom Moses in the law, and the prophets did write as the Messiah; and whom the evangelists and apostles proclaimed as the divine Redeemer and Lord of men. AMEN.

THE FIRST COMING.

THE FIRST COMING.

"When the fulness of the time was come, God sent forth his Son, made of a woman, made under the law, to redeem them that were under the law."—GAL. 4: 4.

"Christ, by highest heaven adored;
Christ, the Everlasting Lord;
Late in time, behold Him come,
Offspring of the virgin's womb.
Veiled in flesh, the Godhead see;
Hail, the Incarnate Deity!
Pleased, as man, with men to dwell,
Jesus, the Immanuel!"

THE great Hope set before men, in the Old Testament, was the coming of the Messiah. As the bow in the cloud, when the storm is past, stretches from horizon to horizon, so this hope spanned, with its beauty and power, the whole period from Eden to Bethlehem. It sprang up out of that gra-

cious promise of God, so strangely yet sig-
nificantly wrought into the curse upon the
serpent, after the fall.   It became a most
wondrous historic fact, by the birth of Jesus
Christ, the Son of Mary, and the Son of God.

REVELATION PROGRESSIVE.

Divine Revelation was progressive. Its
first rays were few and dim.   They cast, indeed, a blessed gleam upon One who should
be the seed of the woman, but who, notwith-
standing this, in the terrific conflict just then
begun, would at length conquer.   As the
centuries rolled on the sacred light shone
clearer, fuller, brighter. It brought gradually
into view all the varied and marvellous
aspects of the character and work of Him
who was to be, not only the Bruiser of
the serpent, but also the Bringer of Rest ;
the Redeeming Angel ; the revered and
world-ruling Shiloh ; the Stone and Shepherd of Israel ; the Captain of the Lord's
Host ; the Root and the Offspring of David ;

the Wonderful; the Counsellor; the Mighty God; the Everlasting Father; the Prince of Peace; the Lord our Righteousness; the Messenger of the Covenant; or, putting the immense meaning of all these names into one—the Messiah.

PROPHETIC VISION.

By the godly of the former dispensations, the coming of the Messiah was doubtless conceived of as one coming. They saw, indeed, the differing and often antagonistic features of His presence and action among men, as delineated by the prophets; but, to their view, those features were intermingled. Distance shortened, or altogether effaced the perspective. When from a remote point we look upon the mountains, they seem as if in contact. Base crowds upon base; peak touches peak. In fact, they are separate, often, by wide intervals. Ascend the range which is nearest, and from its top you learn that what seemed a part of it is afar off.

So when the ancient prophets, in the light of the Lord, looked into the future, it was like looking upon the mountains. The great events embosomed there appeared contiguous, side by side. There was but little, if any, discernible distance between them. As, however, in the flow of time, prophecy has become history, those events have proved to be successive; often, remote, each from the other. Isaiah and Daniel, for instance, had most impressive visions of things then to come. They saw the Messiah. They saw Him—now in His humiliation, despised and rejected of men, and led in silence as a lamb to the slaughter. They saw Him—now in His glory as a mighty King, the joy of His true subjects, and triumphing over all His foes. It was, however, as if in one and the same picture. Its dark shades and its glowing lights were blended. No clearly defined, much less long interval, was apparent between the altar and the throne; the cross and the crown. With us, Calvary is in the far past; the millennial conquests and glories are yet to come.

AMONG THE GENTILES.

Nor was this great Hope limited to the worshippers of Jehovah. In the substance of it, it had a place and power among the Gentiles. As the families of men increased and went out in separate and diverging lines from the original home of the race, they carried with them the memories of the lost paradise. Among the most vivid of those memories was that promise of Jehovah Elohim—the Lord God, of the victory, at length, over the serpent, the prime deceiver and destroyer, by the seed of the woman, the most gracious and powerful restorer ; that, however long and fierce the battle might be, Immanuel should win it. The golden age with which the world began had indeed vanished away, but from the ruins around them, they looked hopefully forward to a golden age in the future. Doubtless, as one generation after another came and went,

this hope as resting on a divine promise grew
more and more indefinite and feeble, but then
necessity took the place of promise.   Human
needs became great and most urgent.   The
consciousness, also, of creature impotence became complete.   God alone could save.   The
Gentiles as well as the chosen people were
compelled to look upward.   Socrates and
Plato, the peers of the mightiest in intellect,
confessed that help must come from a Divine
One.   Before the last of the Hebrew prophets,
the hope of Israel was also the desire of the
nations.   This deep feeling ripened into
strong faith and intense expectation.   As the
Christian era drew nigh, men everywhere were
intent on what should come.   In the West, Vir-
gil sung of the last time of the Cumean Sibyl,
as present; of a new order of the ages just at
hand; of a new progeny about to descend
from the skies and bring back the reign of
truth and right.   All through the East, as
Tacitus and Suetonius relate, the nations were
looking for some extraordinary person to arise

in Judea and sway the sceptre of the world.
In Jerusalem, that earthly centre of the most
sacred memories and hopes, devout souls like
Simeon and Anna were daily waiting for the
consolation of Israel. From their distant
home, near the Euphrates, or perhaps in
Persia, the Magi actually came to the covenant land with costly gifts and profound
homage for the new-born King.

THE SIGNS FULFILLED.

We can see that precisely then the signs
of this great event, as foretold by the prophets,
had become, or were visibly becoming histori-
ical facts. The Tabernacle of David was fallen
down. The memorable weeks of Daniel drew
near to their close. The second temple was
still standing but would presently be destroyed.
The sceptre was departing from Judah, and a
Lawgiver from between His feet. What of
regal and legislative power still remained to
the Jews was wielded by Herod, an Edomite
and a tyrant. He had the name, and sur-

rounded himself with all the pageantry of a king, but he was dependent upon the will and power of Rome. The coin, current among the people for secular uses, bore the image and superscription of Cæsar. Soon after Herod's death, Palestine was made a province of the iron empire. So clearly was it the fulness of the time.

CHARACTER OF THE COMING.

At an early period intelligent faith discerned that, while the Messiah was to be the seed of the woman, He was also to be immensely more. Eve herself had a glimpse of the wondrous fact, when she exclaimed, " A man, Jehovah !" Isaiah declared no unknown truth when he said, " Thou shalt call his name Immanuel ;" nor Micah when he wrote : " Whose goings forth have been from of old, from everlasting ;" nor Zechariah, when he foretold that Jehovah of Hosts would cry, "Awake, O sword, against the man that is my fellow." Upon this most august Being — divine-human — the faith and hope of many ages fixed with an unyielding grasp. Such an One it was, allied both to earth and heaven, who would come as the Deliverer. How would He come? How did He come? The fact corresponded literally with the prediction.

NOT ONLY ESSENTIAL.

He came not only in His essential presence. By this presence He is everywhere, in all worlds; through all duration. He was thus in the world from the day of its birth, as He will be in it until the day of its doom, filling all space and encompassing all being.

NOR ONLY PROVIDENTIAL.

He came not only in His providential presence. By this presence also, He is everywhere. Having made the worlds and the things which are in them, He constantly upholds and governs what He made; pervading and energizing all nature; maintaining and operating all law ; directing and controlling all events.

He came not only in His spiritual presence. In this sense, too, He was in the world from the beginning until the flood, striving with the wicked ; imparting life and strength to the godly, and working in all men salutary convictions of sin and righteousness.   In this sense He was in the world all the period after the flood, from Noah to Malachi ; and from Malachi to the beginning of the Gospel.   He wrought faith in the patriarchs.   He gave the spirit of law and government to Moses ; of mighty valor to Joshua ; of righteous judgment to Samuel ; of unequaled song to David. It was He, by His Holy One, in the prophets of Israel and Judah, who stimulated their individual life and power as men of God, and fitted them for the noblest service in connection with His truth and His kingdom.

NOR ONLY SYMBOLICAL.

He came not only in His symbolical presence. In the earlier ages, when the written Word was not yet given, or was only in its beginning, He made Himself known, from time to time, to His people, in fitting and significant forms visible to their sight; as in the sword-like flame at Eden; as a man to Abraham in Mamre, and to Jacob at Peniel; as a mighty warrior to Joshua, near Jericho; and as the angel of the Lord to Manoah and his wife, among the Danites. All these appearances, and others like them, were theophanies—manifestations of God. They were real and supernatural, but they were symbolic and transient. They occurred in seasons of exigency. They served special purposes in the divine administration. They were all foreshadows of something better and more glorious in the time to come. They were made by Him, whom the saints in those ages knew as the Jehovah-angel, or the angel of the covenant.

BUT IN THE FLESH.

He came by incarnation. The Eternal Father prepared for Him a body. He took into union with Himself our nature, and brought himself into our essential condition. His coming was literal, visible, personal. The record is no more amazing than it is explicit. " In the beginning was the Word, and the Word was with God, and the Word was God. The same was in the beginning with God. All things were made by Him, and without Him was not anything made that was made. In Him was life, and the life was the light of men. And the Word was made flesh, and dwelt among us, full of grace and truth." " When the fulness of the time was come, God sent forth His Son made of a woman, made under the law." " Who being in the form of God, thought it not robbery to be equal with God, but made Himself of no reputation ; and took upon Him the form of a servant, and was made in the likeness of men, and being found in fashion as a man He humbled Himself, and became obedient unto death ; even the death of the cross:" (John 1 : 1–14 ; Gal. 4 : 4 ; Phil. 2 : 6–8.) Men saw Him in the weakness of infancy. They saw Him grow in stature and in knowledge. They saw Him in Judea, in Samaria, in Galilee, in the coast of Tyre and Sidon, going about doing good; speaking most gracious words, and performing most mighty works. They saw Him tempted in the wilderness ; asleep in the ship on Gennesaret ; weary at the well in Sychar ; a-hungered by the wayside from Bethany ; in tears at the grave of Lazarus. They saw Him in agony in the garden ; in the sharp pains of death on the cross ; and buried in the new tomb of Joseph, which was hewn out in a rock. In the body which God prepared Him, He lived, labored, suffered, died, rose again, and ascended on high, whence He came, leading captivity captive.

RESULT.

Thus, in exact agreement with the voices of
prophecy through the centuries before, and
with the resulting hope of the people of God,
the long-looked for Messiah came.   His coming formed an epoch.   It was the goal of all
the then past; it was the starting-point of all
the then future.   Then, however, was seen
what had not been seen distinctly until then.
From the summit thus gained, men discovered
that what from a distance had seemed to be a
part of it, was in fact, another summit farther
off.   They discovered that an interval, filled
with most interesting and vital things, lay
between the humiliation and the glory of the
Messiah; that instead of intermingling, as
had been the appearance in the prophetic panorama, they were separate and distinct, each
having not only its own special characteristics,
but also its own special period.   All that which
had been foretold of the former was indeed
now signally fulfilled.   Not one word which

"holy men spake as they were moved by the Holy Ghost," when "they testified beforehand, the sufferings of Christ," fell to the ground. "He was in the world, and the world was made by Him, and the world knew Him not. He came unto his own, and his own received Him not." "He spake as never man spake," confirming his incomparable words by many undeniably divine works, but in vain with reference to the mass of men. Having eyes they saw not, and having ears they heard not; neither would they understand with their heart and be converted. Expressing his estimate of human character, Cicero had said that if perfect excellence could be embodied, or become incarnate, the world would bow down and worship. The great Roman orator was wholly mistaken. In the Messiah, perfect excellence had visible embodiment; and yet from His birth in Bethlehem to His death on the cross, men and devils combined to make his life one of trial and sorrow. When He publicly entered upon His unexampled mission as the

Saviour of men, Jews and Gentiles alike de-
rided His claims and rejected His message.
" The kings of the earth stood up, and the
rulers were gathered together against the Lord
and against his Christ." Pharisees and Sad-
ducees, scribes and priests were as one man in
their will and efforts to put Him to shame before the people, and bring discredit on His
character, His teaching and His works. The
fearful climax was reached, when with loud
voices the furious crowd demanded of Pilate,
" Crucify Him! crucify Him!" and that crime
without a parallel was done. See them:

> " See how his back the scourges tear,
>   Unto the bloody pillar bound ;
> The ploughers make long furrows there,
>   Till all his body is one wound.
>
> In scorn they robe Him, crown, adore,
>   In spite they rend His robe away ;
> They crush Him with that burden sore,
>   They drag Him up the accursed way,
>
> His sacred limbs they stretch, they tear,
>   With nails they fasten to the wood ;
> His sacred limbs exposed and bare,
>   Or only covered with His blood.

Behold His temples crowned with thorn,
   His bleeding hands spread out so wide;
His streaming feet transfixed and torn,
   The fountain gushing from His side.

Where is the King of Glory now?
   The everlasting Son of God?
The Immortal hangs His languid brow;
   The Almighty faints beneath the load."

Most utter humiliation of the Messiah! What bitterer ingredient could be added to His cup of suffering and shame? It did not however deter Him, nor did it surprise Him. He foreknew it all from the eternal years and made haste to meet it. Most freely He chose it all, rather than that Satan should triumph and men should perish. It had its firm place in the covenant of peace between the Father and the Son. It was there as a condition of the promised glory. It was thus He laid the broad and deep foundation of that glory. In this way it was He finished the transgression, sealed up sins from the sight of God, made reconciliation for iniquity, and brought in the everlasting righteousness. By means of the cross, He won the crown.

3

INFERENCE.

Nor can it be reasonably doubted, that the absolutely literal fulfilment of everything which the sure word of prophecy foretold of the low estate of Him who was to come, invests with certainty a like fulfilment of everything which the same sure word foretells of Him as the world-wide Conqueror and the King of Kings. God himself has given us the true principle of prophetic fulfilment, and therefore of prophetic interpretation, in the palpable and amazing facts of history. Who will dare affirm, in respect to this matter, that the future will be the reverse of the past, or out of analogy with it ; or that the past misleads and deceives men as to the future ? No conceivable presumption against any prophecy now unfulfilled can be so extreme as was that against the incarnation and the death of the Messiah, who, though the Son of Man, was also the Son of God. But the incarnation and the death have taken place. They have

their record as undeniable, unexampled, everlasting realities. The Messiah was born, and
He died. As certainly He will triumph and
gloriously reign.

"God with us! Oh, glorious name !
 Let it shine in endless fame ;
 God and man in Christ unite ;
 Oh ! mysterious depth and height!

 God with us! the Eternal Son,
 Took our soul, our flesh, our bone;
 Now, ye saints, His grace admire,
 Swell the song with holy fire.

 God with us! but tainted not
 With the first transgressor's blot;
 Yet He did our sins sustain,
 Bear the guilt, the curse, the pain.

 God with us! Oh, wondrous grace!
 Lo! we see Him face to face,
 Now, Immanuel we may sing,
 Gracious Saviour, glorious King ! "

THE COMING AGAIN.

THE COMING AGAIN.

" Unto them that look for Him shall He appear the second time, without sin, unto salvation."—HEB. 9: 28.

" On His shoulder He shall bear
Power and majesty; and wear
On His vesture and His thigh,
Names most awful, names most high.

Wonderful in counsel He;
Christ, the Incarnate Deity;
Sire of Ages, ne'er to cease,
King of Kings, and Prince of Peace."

THE great Hope set before men in the New Testament is the coming again of the Messiah; or, using the Greek form of the word — The Christ. The two words are one in meaning, and denote in the Scriptures the same person. The Messiah of the law and the prophets is the Jesus Christ of the evangelists and the apostles. Paul, therefore, upon his conversion, preached Jesus, that He is the Son of God; that the Messiah must needs die and rise again; and that Jesus is He. So far as the person is concerned, all that the Old Testament made known as to the then coming One has its realization in Him who was born in Bethlehem of Judea. Having sanctified infancy and childhood by being Himself an infant and a child; having then been inaugurated in His public office and work as the Messiah, by the descent upon Him of the Spirit as a dove at the Jordan, and by the voice from the heavenly glory, saying, "This is my beloved Son, in whom I am well pleased, hear ye Him;" having also overcome in that dire temptation, to which as the second Adam, He was subjected at the outset of His course; having, moreover, shed the true light upon men by means of His simple yet marvellous teachings of grace and truth, and set before them the one perfect example of a perfect life; having likewise, through the Eternal Spirit, offered Himself on Calvary without spot unto God, the appointed sacrifice for the sins of men, and come forth alive again from the grave where weeping love laid Him, He ascended from the Mount of Olives, in divine array, to the glorious high throne of the Father. From thence He now exercises, invisibly to us, supreme and universal dominion; for " The Lord said unto my Lord, sit Thou at' my right hand until I make thine enemies thy footstool." His next great Messianic manifestation is to be His return from that throne to this world, in glory and for judgment.

ANCIENT INTIMATIONS.

In the visions of the prophets, as already noted, the great events connected with the Messiah appeared to be grouped, having their place or time near together. Those which were the most remote crowded close upon those which were nearest. It is certain, how-

ever, that the saintly ones of the former dispensations were not without the essential
truth.   All the great characteristics of the
two comings they had in clear view; they did
not have the true and full perspective.   They
saw the sufferings and they saw the glory;
they did not see the momentous and prolonged interval between them.   They had the
precious substance of the truth, without its
chronology; we have the chronology and the
substance.   It cannot be without interest or
spiritual use to mark how from the beginning
the second coming of the Messiah has been
an essential part of the faith once for all delivered to the saints.   Like a line of living
light, it has shone across the ages.

BEFORE THE FLOOD.

Go back to Eden.   While Adam and Eve
yet linger there, note that germinal promise.
" He shall bruise thy head," said the Lord God
to the serpent; *i.e.*, in the dread conflict now
begun He shall subject thee to utter and end-

less overthrow. The Lord has come once on the wings of love, and returned again to his Father's side; but this conflict is still in progress; this victory is yet in the womb of the future. The battle will be ended and the victory forever won only when the Lord shall again come in robes of judgment. (Gen. 3 : 15).

Hearken also to Enoch, the seventh from Adam. What startling words he pours forth on the ears of his generation. " Behold," he cries, " the Lord cometh with ten thousand of his saints to execute judgment on all the ungodly, and to convince all that are ungodly among them of all their ungodly deeds which they have ungodly committed, and of all their hard speeches which ungodly sinners have spoken against Him." This was not fulfilled by the flood. The Lord did not then come with myriads of His saints. Nor was it fulfilled by the birth in Bethlehem. Rejoicing angels were indeed there, but the Lord did not then come in judgment. He came to seek and to save the lost. The eye of Enoch was fixed upon the second coming: "When the Lord Jesus shall be revealed from heaven, with His mighty angels, in flaming fire, taking vengeance." So "Jude, the servant of Jesus Christ, and the brother of James," certifies; and he therefore makes use of this prophecy to admonish all the ungodly now, "who turn the grace of God into lasciviousness, and deny the only Lord God, and our Lord Jesus Christ."

TO THE PATRIARCHS.

Come down the interval from Enoch to Abraham. Time and again he heard the voice of Jehovah, addressing to him words of counsel or of promise. Time and again he saw the Angel of Jehovah, in visible form and act. On some occasion, when or how is not revealed, he also saw the day of Christ. Our most gracious Saviour affirms it. What day of Christ? Perhaps the words were meant to cover the whole period bounded by the two comings. It is observable, however, that in the usage of the New Testament

the day of Christ denotes, not the day of His
weakness, but of His power ; not the day of
His sorrow, but of His joy ; not the day of
His deep suffering and shame, when men
mocked at Him, but of His glorious manifestation, when they will cry, " Crown Him ! " And
most certain it seems that the vision of the
patriarch embraced that still future time when
this vast promise shall reach its fulfilment :
" In thy seed shall all the nations of the earth
be blessed, because thou hast heard my voice."
(1 Cor. 1 : 9 ; Phil. 1 : 10 ; Gen. 22 : 18).

From Beersheba cross the desert into Egypt.
The aged Jacob is there, not only to see
and be cared for by his long-mourned Joseph,
but, also, in the purpose of God, to die. The
mortal hour is visibly at hand. His sons
gather at his couch. What gleams from above
lighten that home in Goshen, and turn the
death-scene into one of glory. What an apocalypse of things to come touching the tribes of
Israel ; and especially touching the promised
seed ! The sceptre and the law, he cries, will

linger in Judah until Shiloh comes.   This was
fulfilled at the incarnation.   But centuries beyond this pass before the dying seer.   Far
down the track of time he sees the Redeemer
—not crucified, but enthroned by the nations.
This world-wide obedience ; this reverent and
adoring homage are yet in the future.

IN THE PSALMS.

Listen also to David, the son of Jesse—the
man who was raised up on high, the anointed
of the God of Jacob and the sweet Psalmist
of Israel.   Looking on Calvary, and personat-
ing the Messiah, hear him cry :

> " The dogs have compassed me.
> The assembly of the wicked have enclosed me.
> They pierced my hands and my feet.
> I may tell all my bones.
> They look and stare upon me.
> They part my garments among them,
> And cast lots upon my vesture." (Psalms 22 : 16-18).

Behold, however, another scene :

> " Why do the heathen rage,
> And the people imagine a vain thing ?
> The kings of the earth set themselves,

And the rulers take counsel together,
Against the Lord, and against His Anointed, saying:
Let us break their bands asunder,
And cast away their cords from us.

He that sitteth in the heavens shall laugh;
The Lord shall have them in derision,
Then shall He speak unto them in His wrath,
And vex them in His sore displeasure.
Yet have I set my King upon my holy hill of Zion.

I will declare the decree,
The Lord hath said unto me, thou art my Son;
This day have I begotten Thee.
Ask of me and I shall give thee the heathen for
    thine inheritance,
And the uttermost parts of the earth for thy possession.
Thou shalt break them with a rod of iron;
Thou shalt dash them in pieces like a potter's vessel.

                                    (Psalms 2: 1-9).

And when this work of judgment is past, Behold the King!

" He shall have dominion from sea to sea,
  And from the river unto the ends of the earth.
  They that dwell in the wilderness shall bow before Him;
  And His enemies shall lick the dust.
  The kings of Tarshish and of the Isles shall bring presents,.
  Yea, all kings shall bow down before Him.
  All nations shall serve him."
" His name shall endure forever.
  His name shall be continued as long as the sun;
  All men shall be blessed in Him;
  All nations shall call Him blessed." (Psalms 72: 16-18).

THROUGHOUT THE PROPHETS.

Where can we find grander themes or sublimer strains than in the writings of those extraordinary men the Hebrew prophets? Nay, in all literature besides, where are their equals for thoughts that breathe and words that burn? Not fable, not fiction, not the things which are seen and temporal, engage and engross them. Their sphere of mental sight and foresight is within the real; the moral and spiritual; the eternal. They tell of truth and righteousness; of sin and judgment; of the divine counsels and acts; of the everlasting verities. Consult their pages with reference especially to the coming One. What surpassing scenes! what contrasts of character and condition! what intermingling of lights and shades! Here what gloom! there what glory!

ISAIAH.

Turn to Isaiah the son of Amoz; whose lips one of the cherubim touched with the living coal from off the altar.

He set forth the humiliation of the Messiah,
with the fulness and vividness almost of the
Gospels. He saw Him as a child born ; as a
tender plant out of dry ground, without form
or comeliness ; His visage was so marred more
than any man ; and His form more than the
sons of men. He saw Him despised and rejected by those whom He came to save ; a
man of sorrows and familiar with grief ;
wounded for our transgressions, and bruised
for our iniquities ; bearing thus that moun-
tain-like burden which Jehovah laid upon Him.
He saw Him taken from prison and from
judgment ; brought as a lamb to the slaughter ;
cut off out of the land of the living, and having His grave with the wicked, and with the
rich in His death. All this passed before the
vision of the prophet ; and all this became
history at the first coming.

But, note now another scene. Blending
with this picture, or gleaming across its back-
ground, what a strange contrast. The just
now oppressed and slain One, becomes a

4

mighty King.   He puts on righteousness as a
breast-plate and an helmet of salvation upon
His head.   He is glorious in His apparel and
travels in the greatness of His strength.   He
treads the wine-press alone, and of the people
there are none with Him.   He treads them in
His anger, and tramples them in His fury, and
their blood is sprinkled upon all His raiment.
The day of vengeance is in His heart, and the
year of His redeemed is come.   Out of Zion
goes forth the law, and the Word of the Lord
from Jerusalem.   The mountain of the Lord's
house is established in the top of the mountains, and exalted among the hills, and all the
nations flow unto it.   The moon is confounded
and the sun is ashamed when the Lord of Hosts
reigns in Mount Zion, and before His ancients
gloriously.   Can there be a doubt that all this
is to be realized at the second coming ? (Isaiah
53 : 1–9 ; 32 : 1 ; 59 : 17 ; 63 : 1–4 ; 2 : 2, 3 ; 24 :
23.)

JEREMIAH.

Jeremiah was the prophet of sorrow. His heart was broken within him, and his eyes ran down with tears because of the sins of his people, and the fearful desolation about to overwhelm them. His prophecies resound with no exulting joy in view of the first coming of the Messiah. He glances indeed at that scene in Ramah, and weeps aloud with Rachel weeping for her children, and would not be comforted, because each was not; and then his vision sweeps down those long centuries, still in progress, of the dispersion and affliction of Israel and Judah. Were there ever sights more sad and woful? These centuries do, indeed, at length end; and the prophet sees and hails the Divine Restorer. His plaintive harp vibrates with a song of gladness. Hear it.

" Behold the days come, saith the Lord, that I will raise unto David a righteous branch, and a king shall reign and prosper, and shall exe-

cute judgment in the earth. In His day Judah
shall be saved, and Israel shall dwell safely ; and
this is His name whereby He shall be called,
The Lord our righteousness. Therefore, behold, the days come, saith the Lord, that they
shall no more say, the Lord liveth which
brought up the children of Israel out of Egypt ;
but, the Lord liveth which brought up and
which led the seed of the house of Israel, out
of the North country; and from all the countries whither I had driven them ; and they
shall dwell in their own land." (Jer. 31 : 15 ;
23 : 5–8 ; 33 : 14–17.)

Mark the terms of this prophecy. They
point as with a sunbeam to the Messiah in the
day of His regal power. The facts of history
compel us to the future for its fulfilment. Is
the Messiah now a King ? So He is, but invisibly to men, and disowned and rejected by
them. Was there a return from Babylon ?
So there was ; but, at best, it was partial, and
not to be compared with the exodus from
Egypt, in numbers, or in the manifestations

of Jehovah's grace and might.   Did the Messiah come by incarnation at Bethlehem ?   So He did ; but, then Judah was not saved, nor did Israel dwell safely.   They were overshadowed and oppressed by the all-crushing power of Rome.   The times of the Gentiles had begun their course.   Through all the centuries since, Jerusalem has been trodden down of the Gentiles, and the Jews have been scattered over all the earth.   It will continue to be so, both as to the Holy City, and the covenant land and people, until the times of the Gentiles are fulfilled.   (Luke 21 : 24.)

EZEKIEL.

Among the captives in Babylon, by the river of Chebar, was Ezekiel, a priest, the son of Buzi.   Though later in the prophetic office than Jeremiah, he was like him deeply moved by the sins and the doom of his people.   His visions of God, unique in form and largely impressed by the scenes around him, embrace in their reach some of the vast things of the

future. Plainly there fell upon his eye the
light of the two comings. He saw the highest branch of the highest cedar — a tender
one—planted in the mountain of the height
of Israel. He also saw the diadem taken from
that profane and wicked prince, whose day
was even then come, and after mighty over-
turnings, given to Him whose right it is. He
saw, moreover, not only a restoration from
Babylon, but the restoration of the outcasts
of Israel, and of the dispersed of Judah, out
of all the countries where they are scattered ;
when they shall no more be two nations, but
one ; and one king shall be to them all ; and
David shall be their king ; and they shall walk
in the statutes and judgments of the Lord
their God, and do them ; and He will make a
covenant of peace with them, an everlasting
covenant ; and He will place them and multi-
ply them, and set His sanctuary in the midst
of them forevermore ; and God will be their
God, and they shall be His people ; when
also this great promise shall have its perfect ful-

filment, " Then will I sprinkle clean water upon you, and ye shall be clean ; from all your filthiness, and from all your idols I will cleanse you. A new heart also I will give you; and a new spirit will I put within you; and I will take away the stony heart out of your flesh, and I will give you a heart of flesh." Likewise, in the visions of God, the prophet saw that wonderful symbolic temple into which the glory of the Lord came, by the way of the gate toward the East, and the glory of the Lord filled it; and that equally wonderful symbolic city, whose name shall be Jehovah Shammah; The Lord is there! Where, either since or before the incarnation, has all this been realized? Does it not remain to bless and glorify the future? (Ezek. 17 : 22–24; 21 : 26; 37 : 22–28; 39 : 25; 43 : 4; 48 : 35).

DANIEL.

When we turn to the man greatly beloved, illustrious as a statesman as well as a prophet, intimately conversant with secular as well as

sacred affairs, we find most definite views of
Messiah the Prince, both in His weakness and
in His power.   Daniel saw the Anointed, the
Christ in His first coming.   He saw Him at
the very crisis of His passion ; dying just when
Israel would be expecting Him to reign ; cut off
by a death of violence, not, indeed, for Himself.
His death was a substitution and an expiation.
It made an end of sins for all who put their
trust in Him.   It brought in for their pardon
and complete salvation a righteousness, in its
value without limit, and in its duration without
end.   But from this astonishing scene on Calvary the eye of the prophet glanced far forward.   It fixed with intent gaze on the most
distant future as yet revealed.   Already the
throne of David was fallen down with the fall
of Zedekiah ; and it was to remain abased until the true Heir should come.   Already had
Ezekiel seen the glory of the Lord depart
from the threshold of the temple, and from
the midst of the city ; and Jerusalem was no
more His dwelling place.   The God of heaven

had turned to the Gentiles. He had given to Nebuchadnezzar a kingdom, power, strength and glory. He had appointed him as the head of those great world-powers, which should continue for ages, and which were symbolized, as to character and succession, by a huge metallic image, shown to the monarch of Babylon in a vison of the night. Gentile supremacy and the times of the Gentiles began with him. But lo! this colossal image, suddenly falls. A stone cut out of the mountain without hands—the stone of Israel, which the builders rejected—smites it, and destroys it. Not, however, let it be noted, at the first coming. That was the day of grace and truth, of divine sorrow and measureless love. The stone smites the image—not upon its head of gold ; nor upon its breast and arms of silver; nor upon its belly and thighs of brass ; nor upon its legs of iron ; but upon its feet of iron and clay. It smites it therefore when the fourth kingdom symbolized in the image has reached its last form and been divided in-

to ten kingdoms. In the days of these kingdoms, and as we now know, in their last days,
will the stone that smites them, break them
in pieces, take their place, filling the whole
earth, and the God of heaven set up a kingdom that shall be invincible and indestructible.
Moreover, Daniel " Beheld, till the thrones
were placed, and the Ancient of days did sit,
whose garment was white as snow, and the
hair of His head like wool; His throne was
like the fiery flame, and his wheels as a burning fire. A fiery stream issued and came
forth from before Him; thousand thousands
ministered unto Him, and ten thousand times
ten thousand stood before Him; the judgment was set and the books were opened."
And then " Behold, one like the Son of Man,
came with the clouds of heaven, and came to
the Ancient of days, and they brought Him
near before Him, and there was given Him
dominion and glory, and a kingdom, that all
people, nations, and languages should serve
Him. His dominion is an everlasting dominion,

which shall not pass away; and His kingdom
that which shall not be destroyed." This
fatal smiting of the great image; this dread
judgment before the Ancient of days, this
glorious dominion of one like the Son of
Man, still await historic realization. (Ezek.
10: 18; 11: 23; Dan. 9: 24–26; 2: 31–45;
7: 13.)

THE MINOR PROPHETS.

In the minor prophets the essential facts
are the same. Many a sacred ray shoots
across their pages, revealing the Messiah at
His first coming. They set forth His divine
nature, and yet recognize him as the Son of
David. They tell how the nations will be
yearning, consciously or unconsciously for
His advent, because of the miseries which are
upon them. They point out where He will
be born and within what period. They
announce a messenger to go before Him to
prepare His way; and that He himself will
suddenly come to His temple. They fore-

show His betrayal for thirty pieces of silver,
and that field of blood bought with the
accursed price. They affirm that the sword
of Jehovah will smite Him, though He is
Jehovah's fellow, and that His little ones will
be scattered. But they pass on from the first
advent to the second. They see Him as a
Priest upon His throne, and bearing the
glory; as standing and ruling in the majesty
of the Lord God; as gathering all nations into
the valley of Jehosaphat, and pleading with
them there for His heritage ; as roaring out of
Zion, and uttering His voice from Jerusalem, and then, though the earth and the
heavens shake, as being the hope and the
strength of His people ; as going forth to
fight against the nations which encompass
Jerusalem in array of battle ; as standing, in
that day, upon the Mount of Olives, which is
before Jerusalem on the east, and which shall
then cleave in the midst toward the east and
toward the west; and they connect these
stupendous transactions with that time when

the Lord God shall come with all His holy ones. How certain is it, that these prophets revealed amazing events not yet in history? (Mic. 5: 2–4; Hag. 2: 6–9; Zech. 6: 9–13; 11: 12–14; 13: 7; 14: 3–4; Mal. 3: 1.)

THE NEW TESTAMENT.

It is not, however, until after the first coming, and we see in the clearer and fuller light of the New Testament, that we gain the completed view of the second coming. The New Testament has its living root, and its majestic trunk and branches in the Old. The Old Testament has its rich and divine flower and fruit in the New. They are not two separate trees of life from the heavenly Paradise; they are one and the same tree; planted, and from first to last cultured and vivified by the one eternal spirit of God. The Old Testament foretold the Messiah as to come, and shadowed forth the essential qualities of His person, character, office, work, and kingdom. In the New Testament the Messianic prophecy

culminates in visible and marvellous history.
We have the record of the coming, and of
Him who came. Where before there was
only outline, or, at most, grouping without
perspective, there are details, and the true
relations and proportions, and clearer and
fuller vision of the yet future. It is in this
light, therefore, we reach the truth in its com-
pleteness, which, in its substance, was the
heritage of the saints from the beginning.

SEEMING FAILURE.

After a life of about thirty-three years
among men, a life that has no parallel for its
beneficence, and for its moral beauty and
power—the Messiah, or Jesus Christ, was, by
wicked hands, crucified and slain. What an
astonishing event! Instead of honor, men
covered Him with ignominy. Instead of
power, He fell, apparently helpless, before
His enemies. Instead of a world-wide sceptre
and a glorious throne, as the prophets sung,
He went suddenly to the grave, and the grave

of one charged with crime. What wonder if the Scribes and Pharisees exulted over His death, and thought that was the end of Him. What wonder if His little band of disciples was utterly cast down. Certainly, there was this obvious alternative; either the long series of prophecies which went before on the Messiah had largely failed, or He must come again. An intelligent faith would embrace the latter conclusion. To such a faith, that which had taken place, so exact and amazing, would render most certain, the complete fulfilment of that which remained. As He had come and endured all the suffering, sooner or later the glory must follow.

DIVINE SOLUTION.

Our blessed Lord gave intimations of this truth at an early period of His ministry. From time to time afterward, as the disciples were able to bear it, He made it known to them plainly. "Nevertheless," He said, " When the Son of Man cometh, shall He

find faith on the earth?" But the Son of
Man was then with them. His words, therefore, implied that he was to go away, and
come again. Again He said, " When the Son
of Man shall come in His glory, and all the
holy angels with him, then shall He sit upon
the throne of His glory." (Matt. 25 : 31).
The Son of Man was there and then present,
but in a most humble condition. His words
therefore teach that he would come again and
be known and seen in His power and glory as
a king. And so again : " For the Son of Man
shall come in the glory of his Father, with
His angels, and then shall he reward every
man according to his works." (Matt. 16 : 27).
And still again : " In the regeneration," *i. e.*,
in the new world which is to be, " When the
Son of Man shall sit in the throne of His
glory, ye also shall sit upon twelve thrones,
judging the twelve tribes of Israel." (Matt.
19 : 28.) Before the death of our Lord, every
doubt as to this matter was dissipated, and
the disciples were looking forward to the

second coming. When, therefore, a few days before His passion, He sat on the Mount of Olives ˙ with the forsaken and doomed Jerusalem in view, they came to Him with the question : " What shall be the sign of thy coming ; and of the end of the world? " In reply, He uttered that momentous prophecy, which still stands as a beacon light to the Church and the world, and in which He again declared, " Then shall appear the sign of the Son of Man, and then shall all the tribes ot the earth mourn ; and they shall see the Son of Man coming in the clouds of heaven, with power and great glory." (Matt. 24 : 3–10).

RESULT.

It is plain from all this that there is to be a second coming of the Lord, and that this will fill up all the foreshowing of prophecy as to His kingly character and dominion, just as His first coming has filled up all the foreshowing of prophecy as to His being a servant and a sacrifice. In the divine order the cross was

B

to be first; and then, and because of it, the crown.   This order was a necessity.   "Ought not Christ to have suffered these things, He said, and to enter into His glory?" and the heart of those sad ones on the way to Emmaus burned within them as they heard Him. And so again, on the evening of the Ressurrection day, He said to the eleven as they were gathered together : "These are the words which I spake unto you, while I was yet with you, that all things must be fulfilled which were written in the law of Moses, and in the prophets, and in the Psalms, concerning Me.   Then opened He their understanding, that they might understand the Scriptures, and said unto them, Thus it is written, and thus it behoved Christ to suffer, and to rise from the dead on the third day." See those eager disciples!   How their souls catch and fire at the words : " Rise from the dead on the third day !"   Surely it will be to reign !   He will then come in His glory ! He will then, by great acts of power and judgment, overwhelm those who just now rejected and crucified Him, and establish, visibly, His mighty kingdom! No, ye loving and adoring ones. The time is not yet. I have died, and I have come back from the dead, not now to appear in My glory, but that repentance and remission of sins should be preached in My name among all the nations, beginning at Jerusalem!" There must be an interval of patience and mercy. There must be the offer everywhere of the blood-bought salvation. There must be the breaking down of the middle wall of partition which has stood between the Jews and Gentiles for so many ages. There must be the blessed ministrations of the Almighty Spirit, to effect upon men of all races and all climes, the gracious purposes of God in His redeeming Son. There must be the gathering, along successive generations, of that great multitude which no man can number, out of all nations and kindreds, and peoples and tongues, to stand, at length, as conquerors, robed and crowned, before the throne of God and of the Lamb!

UNTIL HE COME.

Without doubt it was a difficult thing for the disciples to adjust their feelings to this fuller revelation. Their love to the person of the Saviour had become most tender and strong, how could they then bear that He should go away from them and remain? In their most sacred beliefs and hopes until now they had held the suffering and the glory of the Messiah to be in close connection, how could they then without a struggle, give up these beliefs and hopes, and see the Name above all Names still contemned and dishonored among men? As the dreaded hour of separation drew nigh they instinctively shrank from it. On the night of the Last Supper sorrow filled their hearts. When at the table the divine Master said: "This is My body which is given for you; do this in remembrance of Me;" and also, "This cup is the New Testament in My blood, which is shed for many, for the remission of sins," who can conceive what thoughts and feelings swept through their souls! But in the darkness a light arises. If the blessed One ordains the Supper for a memorial, He also ordains it for a pledge and a prophecy. If it tells them of His sacrifice, it also tells them of His triumph. Along the coming time, it will indeed point back to Mount Calvary, but it will also point forward to Mount Zion. He made it, there and then, to herald the hope of the Church till he come! Then followed those wondrous discourses. Did mortals ever before listen to such thoughts and truths? Their beauty, spirit, power, must have made that upper room like heaven. To cheer them in their sadness He said: " I tell you the truth ; it is expedient for you that I go away ; for if I go not away the Comforter will not come unto you ; but, if I depart I will send Him unto you, and when He is come, He will reprove the world of sin, and of righteousness,

and of judgment." " He shall glorify Me, for
He shall receive of Mine, and shall show it
unto you." To quicken their hope, and nerve
them for the coming labor and conflict, He
said: "Let not your heart be troubled; ye
believe in God, believe also in Me. In my
Father's house are many mansions, if it were
not so, I would have told you. I go to prepare a place for you. And, if I go and prepare a place for you, I will come again, and
receive you unto Myself, that where I am,
there ye may be also!" Presently, they left
that sacred chamber. They crossed over the
brook Cedron. They went into Gethsemane,
and some of them witnessed the agony there.
On the morrow they saw Him hang in pain
and death on the tree! but, those stirring
words, " I will come again!" sounded on like
a trumpet. In the Acts; in the Epistles; in
the Apocalypse, they ring out, at every now
and then, as a loud voice from heaven, to
rouse and urge onward the sacramental host;
and when the Word of God closes its last

accents are the solemn cry of the Bridegroom,
"Surely I come quickly: Amen!" with the
yearning response of the Bride, "Even so,
come, Lord Jesus!"

"The Church has waited long
   Her absent Lord to see;
And still in loneliness she waits,
   A friendless stranger she.
Age after age has gone,
   Sun after sun has set,
And still in weeds of widowhood,
   She weeps a mourner yet.

We long to hear Thy voice,
   To see Thee, face to face,
To share Thy crown and glory then,
   As now we share Thy grace.
Should not the loving Bride
   The absent Bridegroom mourn?
Should she not wear the weeds of grief
   Until her Lord return?

The whole creation groans
   And waits to hear Thy voice,
That shall restore her comeliness
   And make her wastes rejoice.
Come, Lord, and wipe away
   The curse, the sin, the stain;
Come, make this blighted world of ours
   Thine own fair world again!"

WHEN WILL IT BE?

WHEN WILL IT BE ?

"Looking for that blessed hope, even the glorious appearing of the great God and our Saviour Jesus Christ."— TIT. 2: 13.

"From heaven when Christ came down of old,
    He took our nature poor and low;
He wore no form of angel mould,
    But shared our weakness and our woe.

But, when He cometh back once more,
    Then shall He set His glorious throne,
And earth and heaven shall flee before
    The face of Him who sits thereon.

O! Son of God, in glory crowned,
    The Judge ordained of quick and dead;
O! Son of man, so pitying found,
    For all the tears Thy people shed;

Be with us in that awful hour,
    And by Thy crown and by Thy grave,
By all Thy love and all Thy power,
    In that great day of judgment, save!"

A GLANCE at the circumstances which will attend and signalize the second coming of the Lord, may fitly precede the

consideration of its time.   They will be seen
to be, as set forth by the Spirit of God
through the evangelists and the apostles,
ineffably grand and impressive.

THE SAME JESUS.

Observe the identity of the Person.   It is
He who was born in Bethlehem ; who died on
Calvary ; and who ascended from the Mount
of Olives.   " This same Jesus," said the angelic
ones, " which is taken up from you into heaven,
shall so come, in like manner as ye have seen
Him go into heaven." (Acts 1 : 11).

VISIBLY.

He will come visibly.   " Behold, He cometh
with clouds, and every eye shall see him ; and
they also which pierced Him ; and all the
kindreds of the earth shall wail because of
Him.   Even so.   Amen." (Rev. 1 : 7).

SUDDENLY.

He will come suddenly, when men do not
expect Him.   " For, as the lightning cometh

out of the east and shineth even unto the
west, so shall also the coming of the Son of
Man be." " And as it was in the days that
were before the flood, they were eating and
drinking, marrying and giving in marriage,
until the day that Noah entered the ark, and
knew not until the flood came, and took them
all away, so shall also the coming of the
Son of Man be." (Matt. 24 : 27–37–39).

IN GLORY.

He will come in most glorious array.
" Hereafter, ye shall see the Son of Man
sitting on the right hand of power, and
coming in the clouds of heaven." " When
the Son of Man shall come in His glory, and
all the holy angels with Him, then shall He
sit upon the throne of His glory." " For the
Son of Man shall come in the glory of his
Father, with His angels, and then He shall
reward every man according to his works."
" And He shall send forth His angels with a
great sound of a trumpet, and they shall

gather His elect from the four winds, from
one end of heaven to the other." (Matt. 17 :
27; 24 : 31 ; 25 : 31 ; 26 : 64).

WITH RESURRECTION POWER.

He will come exercising His divine power
of resurrection.   "The Lord himself shall
descend from heaven with a shout ; with the
voice of the archangel, and with the trump of
God ; and the dead in Christ shall rise first,"
"they that are Christ's at His coming."
"Then we which are alive and remain "—
"changed in a moment, in the twinkling of
an eye, at the last trump "—" shall be caught
up together with them to meet the Lord in
the air, and so shall we ever be with the
Lord." (1 Cor. 15: 23, 51 ; 1 Thess. 4 :
16–17).

FOR JUDGMENT.

He will come as the righteous Judge and
King, "to give every man according as his
work shall be;" "tribulation to them that

trouble you; and to you who are troubled rest with us, when the Lord Jesus shall be revealed from heaven, with His mighty angels, in flaming fire, taking vengeance on them that know not God, and that obey not the Gospel of our Lord Jesus Christ, who shall be punished with everlasting destruction from the presence of the Lord and from the glory of His power, when He shall come to be glorified in His saints, and to be admired in all them that believe." (Rev. 22: 12; 2 Thes. 6: 6–10).

How overpowering will be these scenes! What an infinite contrast between them and those of the first coming! Will not every beholder be impelled to cry—

> "Can this be He! once wont to stray
> A pilgrim on the world's highway;
> By power opprest, and mocked by pride;
> The Nazarene! the Crucified!"

THE TIME.

When will the Lord thus come again? It is an inquiry, not only natural, but also

becoming and right. A true interest in the
great event itself will inevitably awaken a like
interest as to its time. Those holy men of
God, therefore, who spake as they were
moved by the Holy Ghost, searched
diligently, even as those who search for
gold, to learn what time, as well as what
manner of time, the Spirit of Christ which
was in them did signify, when it testified
beforehand the sufferings of Christ, and the
glory that should follow. (1 Pet. 1 : 11.)
They searched, indeed, within the limits of'
the divine revelation. For any mortal to
pass beyond those limits is as irreverent
as it is in vain.

ABSOLUTE TIME.

Of the absolute time of the second coming we know nothing. God has revealed
nothing. The times and the seasons are in
His own power. Almost at the close of His
ministry on the earth, the Saviour said : " Of
that day and that hour knoweth no man ; no,

not the angels which are in heaven; neither the Son "; *i. e.*, in His character and office as the divine-human Mediator, " but the Father." This is still true of all men. It is probably still true of all angels. If the Son has now this knowledge, He has not revealed it. In the Gospels, in the Acts, and in the Epistles, all of which have been given to the Church since He spoke these words, and all of which shed a fuller light than before shone on the events to come, there is no exact determination of the time. Nor from the Apocalypse, that wondrous book, which closes the supernatural record, and " which God gave unto Jesus Christ, to show unto His servants things which must shortly come to pass," can we learn at what hour or on what day the Son of Man will come.

RELATIVE TIME.

Of the relative time, however, of the second coming, the Church has knowledge. It has pleased the Father to cast some of the

6

rays of that light which proceeds from His throne, upon, at least, its place in the order of the divine counsels. We know that the Son of Man came in the manner and at the time foretold by the prophets; and that men did unto Him whatsoever they would. We know that we are living in the last days and under the immediate ministration of the Holy Spirit. We know that these days are now far on in their course, so that, on the scale of divine, and probably, of human measurement, the end is nigh. We know that the next great predicted event in the unfolding future, and relative to the Messianic kingdom, is the manifestation of the Son of God in glory and to reign.

THE MILLENNIUM.

Some, indeed, will ask, must not the millennium intervene? The Scriptures do not teach that it must; but, apparently they teach the reverse. What is the millennium? The word itself is made up of two Latin words, and means, literally, a thousand years. A thousand years are a millennium. In Rev. 20: 1–7, the beloved John uses this word in its Greek form to denote a most signal and glorious period in the history of the Church to be realized in the future. If we read his statements, using the word millennium, instead of translating it, it may serve to render more clear and definite our views of His meaning.

"And I saw an angel come down from heaven, having the key of the bottomless pit and a great chain in his hand. And he laid hold on the dragon, that old serpent, which is the Devil and Satan and bound him a millennium, and cast him into the bottomless pit, and shut him up, and set a seal upon him, that he should deceive the nations no more till the millennium should be fulfilled, and after that, he must be loosed a little season. And I saw thrones, and they sat upon them, and judgment was given unto them; and I saw the souls of them that were beheaded for the witness of Jesus, and for the Word of

God, and which had not worshipped the beast, neither His image, neither had received his mark upon their foreheads, or in their hands; and they lived and reigned with Christ a millennium. But, the rest of the dead lived not again until the millennium was finished. This is the first resurrection. Blessed and holy is he that hath part in the first resurrection; on such the second death hath no power, but they shall be priests of God, and of Christ, and shall reign with Him a millennium. And when the millennium is expired Satan shall be loosed out of his prison."

ANALYSIS.

Analysis of this interesting Scripture shows its essential points to be these, viz:

1. The future embosoms a definite and most eminent period which is here called the millennium.

2. At the beginning of the millennium, Satan is to be bound, cast into the abyss and shut

up, so that he can deceive the nations no more, until the millennium is past.

3. In connection with the binding and imprisonment of Satan, the saintly dead, or the dead in Christ, are to live again. Their resurrection is the first resurrection, or the resurrection of the just, or the resurrection unto life. These risen dead are blessed and holy, and as priests of God and of Christ, they are to reign with Him during the millennium.

4. The rest of the dead, *i. e.*, those who are not dead in Christ, will not then live again. They will have no part in the first resurrection. They sleep on in their graves, and over them the second death will have power.

5. At the close of the millennium, Satan is to be let loose again for a little season.

Such is the origin of the term millennium. Such is the inspired view of the notable period which it designates. Very naturally and doubtless with truth, those glowing descriptions which the Scriptures elsewhere give of the future bliss and glory of the Church on earth, are referred by most to the same period, and the word millennium is used to express their immense import.

INSPIRED DESCRIPTIONS.

In. this view of the Apocalypse, the casting down and repression of Satan, the presence and reign of Christ, and the living again and reigning with Him of His saintly ones, bring in the millennium, and constitute its most distinctive and essential features. All its other blessed characteristics will unfold as the choice flower and fruit of the dominion of Christ and His saints. These characteristics are largely set forth by the revealing Spirit ; and especially in the pages of the ancient prophets. They form a picture of surpassing grandeur and beauty. Look at the delineations which follow.

Daniel 7 : 13–16.

" I saw in the night visions, and behold one like unto the Son of Man came with the clouds of heaven, and came to the Ancient of days, and they brought Him near before Him. And there was given Him dominion and glory and a kingdom that all people, nations and languages should serve Him; His dominion is an everlasting dominion which shall not pass away, and His kingdom that which shall not be destroyed."

David, Ps. 2 : 7–10.

' Yet have I set my King upon my holy hill of Zion.
I will declare the decree;
The Lord hath said unto me, thou art My son;
This day have I begotten thee.
Ask of Me, and I shall give Thee the heathen for thine
    inheritance,
And the uttermost parts of the earth for thy possession.
Thou shalt break them with a rod of iron.
Thou shalt dash them in pieces like a potter's vessel.''

Isaiah 25 : 6–9.

" And in this mountain shall the Lord of Hosts make unto all people a feast of fat things; a feast of wines on the lees; of fat things full of marrow; of wines on the lees well refined. And He will destroy in this mountain the face

of the covering cast over all people, and
the vail that is spread over all nations. He
will swallow up death in victory; and the
Lord God will wipe away tears from all
faces ; and the rebuke of His people shall He
take away from off all the earth ; for the
Lord God hath spoken it. And it shall be
said in that day, Lo, this is our God ; we have
waited for Him ; we will be glad and rejoice
in His salvation."

Isaiah 2 : 2–6.

" And it shall come to pass in the last days,
that the mountain of the Lord's house shall
be established in the top of the mountains,
and shall be exalted above the hills, and all
nations shall flow unto it. And many people
shall go and say, Come ye and let us go up to
the mountain of the Lord, to the house of the
God of Jacob, and He will teach us of His
ways, and we will walk in His paths ; for out
of Zion shall go forth the law, and the Word
of the Lord from Jerusalem. And He shall

judge among the nations, and shall rebuke many people; and they shall beat their swords into plowshares, and their spears into pruning hooks; nation shall not lift up sword against nation, neither shall they learn war any more."

Isaiah 35 : 3–10.

" Strengthen ye the weak hands, and confirm the feeble knees. Say ye to them that are of a fearful heart—Be strong, fear not. Behold your God will come with vengeance, even God with a recompense. He will come and save you. Then the eyes of the blind shall be opened, and the ears of the deaf shall be unstopped. Then shall the lame man leap as an hart, and the tongue of the dumb shall sing ; for in the wilderness shall waters break out, and streams in the desert. And the parched ground shall become a pool, and the thirsty land springs of water; in the habitation of dragons, where each lay, shall be grass with reeds and rushes. And an highway shall be there, and a way, and it shall be

called, the way of holiness: the unclean
shall not pass over it; but it shall be for those;
the wayfaring men, though fools, shall not
err therein.   No lion shall be there, nor any
ravenous beast shall go up thereon ; it shall
not be found there ; but the redeemed shall
walk there, and the ransomed of the Lord
shall return and come to Zion with songs and
everlasting joy upon their heads; they shall
obtain joy and gladness, and sorrow and sigh-
ing shall flee away."

Isaiah 60: 15–22.

" Whereas thou hast been forsaken and
hated, so that no man went through thee,
I will make thee an eternal excellency, a joy
of many generations.   Thou shalt also suck
the milk of the Gentiles, and shalt suck the
breast of kings, and thou shalt know that I
the Lord am thy Saviour, and thy Redeemer,
the mighty one of Jacob.   For brass I will
bring gold; and for iron I will bring silver;
and for wood, brass; and for stones, iron.   I

will also make thy officers peace, and thine exactors righteousness. Violence shall no more be heard in thy land, wasting nor destruction within thy borders, but thou shalt call thy walls, salvation, and thy gates, praise. The sun shall no more be thy light by day; neither for brightness shall the moon give light unto thee; but the Lord shall be unto thee an everlasting light, and thy God thy glory. Thy sun shall no more go down; neither shall thy moon withdraw itself; for the Lord shall be thine everlasting light, and the days of thy mourning shall be ended. Thy people also shall be all righteous; they shall inherit the land forever, the branch of my planting, the work of my hands, that I may be glorified. A little one shall become a thousand, and a small one a strong nation. I the Lord will hasten it in its time."

Isaiah 65 : 17–25.

" For behold, I create new heavens, and a new earth; and the former shall not be

remembered, nor come into mind. But, be
ye glad and rejoice forever in that which I
create ; for behold I create Jerusalem a rejoicing, and her people a joy. And I will rejoice
in Jerusalem and joy in my people ; and the
voice of weeping shall be no more heard in
her, nor the voice of crying. There shall be
no more thence an infant of days, nor an old
man that hath not filled his days; for the
child shall die an hundred years old ; but the
sinner being an hundred years old shall be
accursed. And they shall build houses and
inhabit them ; and they shall plant vineyards,
and eat the fruit of them. They shall not
build, and another inhabit; they shall not
plant and another eat; for as the days of a
tree are the days of my people and mine elect
shall long enjoy the work of their hands.
They shall not labor in vain, nor bring forth
for trouble ; for they are the seed of the
blessed of the Lord, and their offspring with
them. And it shall come to pass, that before
they call, I will answer; and while they are

yet speaking I will hear. The wolf and the lamb shall feed together, and the lion shall eat straw like the bullock, and dust shall be the serpent's meat. They shall not hurt nor destroy in all my holy mountain, saith the Lord."

Isaiah 24 : 23.

" Then the moon shall be confounded, and the sun ashamed, when the Lord of Hosts shall reign in Mount Zion, and in Jerusalem and before His ancients gloriously."

Such are some of the delineations of the prophets. In this way do they depict that illustrious period when there shall be given unto One like the Son of Man, dominion and glory and a kingdom. The transcendent vision has kindled the faith and hope of ages in the past. It exerts now a divine power. When men see it turning from prophecy into history they will see the millennium.

VOICE OF THE CHURCH.

" Know ye not that ye are the temple of God," wrote Paul to the Christians in Corinth,

"and that the Spirit of God dwelleth in you ?"
(1 Cor. 3: 16).   It is a glorious truth, the
Spirit of God dwells in the people of God.
But let there be no mistake here.   This
indwelling of the Spirit is not for the purpose
of new revelations of truth ; it is that the
saints may have clearer light upon the truth
already revealed, and that thus they may grow
up into completer holiness.   In proportion as
they are faithful and pure they will have the
light of God, and with joy they will walk in
it.   In the matter of Christian doctrine, therefore, the general sense of the Church ought to
have a special value.   If the Church were
perfect, the creed of the Church would be
the truth.   It is, however, a modifying and
damaging fact, that the Church is not perfect.
Very far from it.   From the beginning, Satan
has assiduously sown his tares among the
good seed of God, and with most sad results.
The test of truth, therefore, is not the voice of
the Church, but the voice of the Bible. " To
the law and the testimony : if they speak not

according to this word it is because there is no light in them." (Isaiah 8: 20).

PRIMITIVE VIEW.

In the apostolic and primitive Church, it is certain that for more than three centuries the second coming of Christ was expected to take place before the millennium, and that the bliss and glory of that period would flow from His presence and reign. Especially was this so while Paganism still held the seat of power, and the Church was despised and persecuted. Most keenly did she then feel the sorrows of widowhood and long for the return of her absent Lord. That return would bring the day of her redemption and joy. When, however, Constantine mounted the throne, and the Church with him, her spirit and her faith changed. Favor with men, and increasing flatteries, honors, wealth and power, made the world seem less barren, and more attractive. Gradually, but surely, the blessed hope gave way to the power of present possession and enjoyment; the once desolate widow became elated, proud, and self-sufficient: and she said in her heart, " I sit as a queen, and shall have no sorrow." For many generations, it would have been the dread of the visible church to have the Lord come.

AFTER THE REFORMATION.

The churches of the Reformation were brought into being by the Spirit through that most vital truth—justification by faith. This engaged their profoundest thought and stirred their deepest feeling. It was, in their view, the very citadel of the whole Christian cause. In some less vital things, their emancipation from Rome was less complete. As to the second coming of the Lord, they did not return wholly to the first faith. In here and there an instance, this faith gained a place in the Confessions, but the general view referred those Scriptures which portray the future dominion and glory of the Church to the state beyond the last judgment; *i. e.,* to

the heavenly and the eternal state. It inter-
posed no millennium before the glorious return of the Saviour. On the contrary, it held
that return to be nigh, even at the door;
but it also held, that it would bring with it
the end of all earthly things. Many, indeed,
of the great theologians of Westminster were
express millennarians; the most of the chief
men among them. They looked first for
Christ to come, and then for His glorious
kingdom. But none in that notable Assembly
knew anything of a latter day of glory to the
Church on earth before the coming of the
Lord. They close, therefore, their grand Confession with the ringing words: "Christ will
have that day unknown to men, that they may
shake off all carnal security, and be always
watchful, because they know not what hour
the Lord will come; and may be ever prepared to say, Come, Lord Jesus, come
quickly. Amen!"

7

MODERN IDEAS.

Those ideas touching the millennium, both
as to its character and time, which have been
generally current within the last century, seem
to have originated with Dr. Daniel Whitby.
Certainly he gave them form and gained for
them attention. Diligent inquirers have not
been able to trace them to any previous
source. By generalizing and spiritualizing
means and processes ; proper, doubtless, in
their due place and measure, he reached the
conclusion that Christ, who was once offered
to bear the sins of many, will not appear the
second time without sin unto salvation, until
after the millennium ; and that this most
signal period in the history of the Church
will be the natural and gradual result of the
intellectual and spiritual agencies now in
existence and operation. The Gospel,
especially, will be more and more widely
preached among the nations ; and the nations
will become more and more subject to its

pervasive and elevating influence, until, like leaven, its sacred force will reach, and more or less mould the whole mass. This was also, and essentially, the view of President Edwards, only he gave more prominence to the work of the Holy Spirit, and His extraordinary manifestations. The great name of Edwards was, deservedly, a power at home and abroad. Sanctioned by so grand a soul, this modern view has taken strong hold upon the Church of the present. The result is, that the Bride is looking and longing, not for the coming of the Bridegroom, which she even denies to be as yet possible ; but, for the coming of the millennium ; a millennium to be realized by means of her own doing, and a millennium without the Bridegroom and the King. At times, she is confident that she sees the first rays of its glory gilding the mountain tops.

THE TRUE WITNESSES.

Where, then, is the truth?   In the Word of God; and, with regard to this matter, only there.   No mere data or process of human reason can furnish its solution.   It belongs to the domain of revealed truth.   If God has made known the relation of the second coming of his Son to the latter day of glory, we must find the knowledge, in the testimony of His witnesses in the Old and the New Testaments.   Let us cite some of these witnesses.   Let us reverently consider their testimony. " The words of the Lord are pure words; as silver tried in a furnace of earth, purified seven times." (Ps. 12: 6).   " Every word of God is pure." (Prov. 30: 5).

Isaiah 25: 6–9.

Listen :

"In this mountain shall the Lord of Hosts make unto all people a feast of fat things; a feast of wine on the lees; of fat things full of marrow, of wines on the lees well refined.   And He will destroy in this mountain the face of the covering cast over all

people, and the vail that is spread over all nations.
He will swallow up death in victory; and the Lord
God will wipe away tears from off all faces; and the
rebuke of His people shall He take away from off all
the earth; for the Lord hath spoken it. And it shall
be said in that day: Lo, this is our God; we have
waited for Him, and He will save us; this is the
Lord; we have waited for Him; we will be glad and
rejoice in His salvation!"

Who can doubt that this prophecy relates
to the times of the Messiah? This mountain
is Mount Zion. The essential preparation for
this notable feast was made by the Lord,
at His first coming, in His life of perfect
obedience, and by His death of atonement on
Calvary. The overspreading vail is that thick
covering, which, with reference to spiritual
things, and by means of ignorance, error, and
sin, Satan has thrown over our race. "The
God of this world hath blinded the minds of
them which believe not, lest the light of the
glorious gospel of Christ, who is the image
of God, should shine unto them." (2 Cor. 4:
3, 4.) While this vail thus covers men, there
can be no millennium. The Lord God,
therefore, will destroy it; and in connection

with this, or in doing it, He will swallow up death in victory.

When will the Lord God do these great things? Let His own most Holy Spirit answer, through the blessed Paul.

> "Behold, I shew you a mystery. We shall not all sleep, but we shall all be changed, in a moment, in the twinkling of an eye, at the last trump; for the trumpet shall sound, and the dead shall be raised incorruptible, and we shall be changed. For this corruptible must put on incorruption, and this mortal must put on immortality. So, when this corruptible shall have put on incorruption, and this mortal shall have put on immortality, then shall be brought to pass the saying, that is written, Death is swallowed up in victory." (1 Cor. 15 : 51–55).

What could be plainer? The Lord God will swallow up death in victory, when "the trumpet shall sound and the dead shall be raised incorruptible." What dead? The apostle leaves no room for doubt. His magnificent discourse relates especially to the resurrection of the dead in Christ; to those who, in their own order, live again at His coming. It is then, therefore, that He will destroy the vail cast over the nations, and pour all abroad the light and glory of the millennium.

Daniel 2 : 31–45.

Again, listen :

" Thou, O King, sawest, and behold a great image. This great image, whose brightness was 'excellent, stood before thee ; and the form thereof was terrible. This image's head was of fine gold ; his breast and his arms of silver ; his belly and thighs of brass ; his legs of iron ; his feet part of iron and part of clay. Thou sawest till that a stone was cut out without hands, which smote the image upon his feet, that were of iron and clay, and brake them to pieces. Then was the iron, the clay, the brass, the silver and the gold, broken to pieces together, and became like the chaff of the summer threshing floors, and the wind carried them away, that no place was found for them ; and the stone that smote the image became a great mountain, and filled the whole earth."

INTERPRETATION.

The prophet now interprets. In this vision God has made known what shall come to pass hereafter. The great image is a symbol. In its form .and materials it represents four mighty kingdoms of this world. They are to

arise, each after the other, and gain wide
dominion. The first is the Babylonian, then
existing. This statement by the prophet
renders it certain that the other three kingdoms are the Medo-Persian, the Macedonian
and the Roman. When the fourth kingdom,
" strong as iron," shall reach a specified stage
in its history, the stone cut out without
hands shall smite the image and destroy it;
and itself will become the world-filling and
world-ruling power; or, " the God of heaven
will then set up a kingdom which shall never
be destroyed; and the kingdom shall not be
left to other people, but it shall break in
pieces and consume all these kingdoms, and it
shall stand forever."

The prophet does not explain the import of
the stone. It was not necessary. It denotes
either " the stone of Israel," rejected by men
but " chosen of God and precious," or, His
Messianic kingdom. Nor does the prophet
determine here the exact time of this kingdom. In the vision itself, however, there are

some interesting and conclusive data. The stone is not to smite and destroy the image, while the fourth kingdom exists in its unity, as it did at the first coming of Christ; nor yet while it exists in its twofold division, as it did in the Eastern and Western empires, represented by the legs of iron ; but, while it shall be existing in its tenfold division, as represented by the feet and toes of iron and clay. The stone will smite upon these, and, destroying the kingdoms which they represent, will bring in their place that kingdom which cannot be destroyed. Demonstrably, therefore, this smiting and this kingdom are yet in the future. At what point in the future ? Let the man greatly beloved answer, in another vision, which he himself saw.

> "I saw in the night visions, and behold, One like the Son of Man came with the clouds of heaven ; and came to the Ancient of days ; and they brought Him near before Him. And there was given Him dominion and glory, and a kingdom, that all people, nations and languages should serve Him ; His dominion is an everlasting dominion, which shall not pass away, and His kingdom that which shall not be destroyed." (Dan. 7 : 12–14).

How impressive is this divine view. How clear the conclusion which it compels. The smiting of the terrible image upon its feet and toes, by the stone ; the destruction of the kingdoms of this world, which these feet and toes symbolize, by this smiting ; and the setting up in their place of that kingdom which shall be everlasting, are plainly contemporaneous events. But this kingdom will be set up, or given to One like the Son of Man, not until He comes with the clouds of heaven ; *i. e.,* at the second coming of Christ. Before that epoch, therefore, there can be no millennium.

Daniel 7 : 2–27.

Hear again the heavenly witness. In this Scripture, we have another prophetic vision. Widely different in form from that of the huge image, it has essentially the same import, only that, in connection with the latter days of the fourth kingdom, it adds some particulars of deep moment. The prophet beholds, coming up from the great sea, four great beasts. The first of these beasts is like a lion, the second like a bear, the third like a leopard, and the fourth--not compared with any other—is exceedingly strong and terrible, and exercises immense powers of destruction. The four great kingdoms set forth in the vision of the image are symbolized here by these four beasts. The extraordinary fourth beast has ten horns. These horns symbolize a tenfold division of the fourth kingdom, just as was done by the ten toes of the image. Among these horns springs up another, a little horn, of a remarkable character. It has eyes, like the eyes of a man ; a mouth speaking great things ; and it plucks up three of the first horns by the roots.

The vision continues " until the thrones were placed, and the Ancient of days did sit, whose garment was white as snow, and the hair of His head like the pure wool. His throne was like the fiery flame, and His wheels as burning fire. A fiery stream issued and came forth from before Him ; thousand

thousands ministered unto Him, and ten
thousand times ten thousand stood before
Him. The judgment was set, and the books
were opened." Up to the very moment of
this overwhelming scene is heard " the voice
of the great words which the horn spake."
But, the judgment proceeds; the beast is slain
and his body given to the burning flame ; the
Son of Man comes with the clouds of heaven,
and is invested by the Ancient of days with
the promised and glorious kingdom.

INTERPRETATION.

Divine manifestations awe men. The
prophet was deeply impressed. His spirit
was troubled within Him. What can this
transcendent vision mean ? Especially did
he desire to " know the truth of the fourth
beast, so diverse from all the others, and
exceedingly dreadful ; and of the ten horns
that were in his head ; and of the other which
came up, and before which three fell ; even of
that horn that had eyes, and a mouth that

spake very great things; whose look was more stout than his fellows; and the same horn that made war with the saints, and prevailed against them." This strong desire of the prophet was answered. " The fourth beast," said the interpreter, "shall be the fourth kingdom upon earth, which shall be diverse from all kingdoms, and shall devour the whole earth, and tread it down and break it in pieces. And the ten horns out of this kingdom are ten kings that shall arise; and another shall rise after them, and he shall be diverse from the first, and he shall subdue three kings. And he shall speak great words against the Most High, and think to change times and laws. And they," *i.e.*, the saints, " shall be given into his hand, until a time and times and the dividing of time."

CONCLUSION.

We have thus the elements of a true and great conclusion. The fourth beast symbolizes the fourth kingdom, *i.e.*, the Roman. Its ten horns symbolize the fourth kingdom in its state of tenfold division, which has existed now for centuries. The little horn, which comes up among the ten, and displaces three of them, symbolizes another kingdom, of a character without its parallel for malignity and impiety. In the light of the past and the present, how can it be doubted that this horn points to the apostate Church—so ambitious of secular as well as ecclesiastical power, and exercising its power all along its course in bitter opposition to the truth and the cause of Christ ? Where else since Constantine does there exist such a record of iniquities and atrocities—for the repression and extirpation, not of evil, but of good; or such an arrogation, by miserable men, of the honors and powers which belong only to God. Beyond any question, this horn designates some formidable and relentless enemy of the saints of the Most High. And now, mark; it makes war with the saints, and prevails against them, and wears them out — how long ? Until the

millennium ?   The inspired answer is : until
the Ancient of days shall come ; until judgment is given to the saints of the Most High ;
until the time is come that the saints possess
the kingdom ; all which events are here in-
separably connected with the coming of the
Son of Man with the clouds of heaven ; or,
what is the same thing, His coming in the
glory of His Father, with all the holy angels.
There can be no millennium, therefore, before
Christ's second coming.

"Far down the ages now,
    Her journey well-nigh past ;
The pilgrim Church fares on, in hope
    To reach the crown at last.

No wider is the gate,
    No broader is the way,
No smoother is the ancient path
    That leads to light and day,

No slacker grows the fight,
    No feebler is the foe,
No less the need of armor tried,
    Of shield and spear and bow.

Nor less we feel the blank
    Of earth's still absent King,
Whose presence is of all our bliss
    The everlasting spring."

QUESTION OF TIME.

(CONTINUED.)

QUESTION OF TIME.

(*CONTINUED.*)

" *Jesus saith unto him, 'Thou hast said; nevertheless, I say unto you, hereafter shall ye see the Son of Man sitting on the right hand of power, and coming in the clouds of heaven.'* "—MATT. 26 : 64.

"How long, O! Lord our Saviour,
  Wilt Thou remain away?
Our hearts are growing weary
  Of thy so long delay;
O! when shall come the moment,
  When brighter far than morn
The sunshine of Thy glory
  Thy people shall adorn.

How long, O! Heavenly Bridegroom,
  How long wilt Thou delay?
And yet how few are grieving
  That Thou dost absent stay.
The very Bride her portion
  And calling hath forgot,
And seeks for ease and glory
  Where Thou, O! Lord, art not.

O ! Wake thy slumbering virgins,
  Send forth the solemn cry,   ·
Let all thy saints repeat it,
  The Bridegroom draweth nigh.
May all our lamps be burning,
  Our loins well girded be,
Each longing heart preparing
  With joy Thy face to see."

A S the witness of the New Testament
     to the second coming of Christ is
more full and definite than that of the Old
Testament with reference to the great event
itself and its accessories, so also it is as to
its time.   It does not, indeed, lift the vail
from "that day and hour" when the Lord
will come, but it pours a clear light on the
divine order.   In harmony with the witness of
the Old Testament, it shows that the great
day of the Lord, when He will come in the
glory of His Father, and with the holy
angels, will precede and usher in the millennium. Glance at some of its testimonies.
Taken singly, they may appear more or less

decisive. Taken together, they lay a solid foundation for Christian faith.

ABSENCE OF THE BRIDEGROOM.

(Matt. 9 : 15.)

John the Baptist was an ascetic. He came neither eating bread nor drinking wine. He was also a preacher of repentance, and enjoined fasting as a religious duty. Like the Pharisees, therefore, his disciples were wont to fast. It was meant to be an expressive, outward sign of strong, inward feeling; a symbolical confession of sin and sorrow; of deep affliction of the soul. The disciples of Jesus did not fast. The fact was observed, and prompted the inquiry, "Why do we and the Pharisees fast oft, but thy disciples fast not?" How instructive and beautiful is the reply: "Jesus said unto them, Can the children of the bride-chamber mourn as long as the Bridegroom is with them?" Certainly not. Well, I am the Bridegroom of the Church. And thus, as Alford points out, He "announces

the fulfilment in Him of a whole cycle of
Old Testament prophecies and figures." And
this being so, how could his disciples fast?
His personal presence with them precluded
sorrow. It did so, even when they saw Him
in the form of a servant, and their knowledge
of Him and His sublime purposes was most
imperfect. Much more will it do this when
He shall be present with them in His full
array of divine beauty and power. "But,"
He added, "the days will come when the
Bridegroom shall be taken from them, and
then shall they fast." The evangelist Luke
has it, "and then shall they fast, in those
days," *i. e.*, when and while the Bridegroom is
gone. The going away of the Bridegroom
was, indeed, expedient; but how the very
thought of it depressed those first disciples.
It would itself be a great sorrow. It would
also bring the season and the occasions for
other sorrows. Then the world would renew
its temptations; then the flesh would stand
disclosed in all its weakness; then Satan

would redouble his infernal craft and power;
then too, if ever, they would know by experience of the great tribulation out of which all
will come who shall stand before the throne
of God and of the Lamb in the glory of conquerors. And how could they suppose the
effect would be less permanent than its cause?
Or, how can we suppose this? The fasting-
time of the Bride is plainly commensurate
with the absence of the Bridegroom; unless,
indeed, meanwhile, her love shall grow cold,
and the Bride become an harlot. But this
would call for still deeper sorrow. It would
indicate anything else than the presence and
glories of the millennium. Those days, therefore, when the Bride shall fast because the
Bridegroom is taken away, will continue until
the Bridegroom returns.

THE DECAY OF FAITH.
(Luke 18: 1–8).

Add to this thought that touching question
of the Lord in the parable of the unjust judge.

He would impress it upon men that they should always pray and not faint. He does this by showing us a widow bringing her suit before an earthly tribunal. The judge is one who does not care for either man or God. His office is his instrument of power and plunder. Time and again, therefore, he sends her from his presence without redress. She, however, will not be denied. She persists in urging and re-urging her case, until the wretch is compelled, by regard to his own ease, to vindicate her. Now, will not God, the infinitely righteous Judge, and who also loves His people with an immeasurable love, hear and answer those who cry day and night unto Him? Most assuredly He will, and that speedily. It may, indeed, sometimes seem to them long that He waits, but their trials and griefs shall be over and gone the first moment their own highest good will permit. This the Scriptures certify, and this the ages have seen. If often the furnace has been exceeding hot, the result in spiritual wealth and beauty has been correspondingly eminent. " Nevertheless," the Saviour proceeds to ask, " when the Son of Man cometh, shall he find faith on the earth?" What a startling inquiry! He will come again, but when He comes, what a spiritual condition of men! It almost overwhelms one to think of it; but the import of the question is plain. Faith will have almost failed when the Son of Man shall come. And yet, the ideas now so current in the Church make this astounding and world-wide decay of faith follow at once upon the millennium; *i. e.*, upon the world-wide prevalence of truth, righteousness, peace, and all the extraordinary blessings and glories of the long-promised thousand years! Is it conceivable? Is it possible? We can, indeed, see how faith in revealed truth may now fail. In fact, we see that it often does fail. In the visible Church itself there seems to be already more of unbelief than of faith. Large numbers of professedly Christian teachers find the ultimate authority in their own reason. Still larger numbers of professedly Christian people delight more in human folly than in the divine wisdom. It is not difficult to believe that in the last days perilous times will come by means of false philosophy, false science, false religion, and of the worldly spirit and unholy lives of those who ought to be the witnesses of God; and that at the end of this dispensation it may be just as it was in the days before the flood. But, that the millennium should come and go and leave no trace behind; that a period which the Scriptures clothe with more than the beauty and brightness of the sun; whose demonstrations of truth will be overwhelming as they will be grand and glorious; whose fruits of righteousness, peace, purity and abounding joy will make the earth again like heaven; and during which "all men shall be blessed in Christ and all nations shall call Him blessed;" that such a period should end in one of almost utter darkness is incredible. For a little season, it is true, Satan will be loosed from his prison.

He will then make another and most desperate attempt against the saints and their mighty King. But with what result? Apparently with no result, except to deceive some of the then unconverted in the four quarters of the earth. Most assuredly there will be no want of faith then in the camp of the saints or in the beloved city. And when at length the great adversary and His embattled host are all ready for the onset, but before they seem to have struck a blow—fire comes down from God out of heaven and devours them. In the Bible view of the future there is no place after the millennium for so stupendous a descent, as the current ideas imply from universal faith and holiness, to universal unbelief and impiety. If, when the Son of Man cometh, He shall not find faith on the earth, His coming must be before the millennium.

THE WHEAT AND THE TARES.

(Matt. 13: 24–30).

Glance also at the parable of the wheat and the tares. Clear and impressive by itself, it

is made specially so by a full interpretation
from the Lord.   The Son of Man sows His
good seed in the visible Church, though, indeed,
not exclusively there ; He sows them, more or
less, through the whole world.   He began this
divine sowing in Eden.   He has continued
His gracious work from that day until now,
and He will continue it until the probation of
men is over.   His great enemy, the devil, is
determined to counteract His efforts, and
frustrate, so far as possible, their beneficent
results.   Broadcast, but by stealth, he sows
tares all over the same field.   Presently, therefore, appear, thoroughly intermingled, the
genuine wheat and the noxious weeds—the
children of the kingdom, and the children of
the evil one.   What now shall be done?
Pluck up and cast away the tares ?   No, says
the Master, " lest ye root up also the wheat
with them.   Let both grow together until the
harvest, and in the time of the harvest I will
say to My reapers, gather ye together first the
tares, and bind them in bundles to burn them,

but gather the wheat into My barn." Verily
His thoughts are not as our thoughts. But,
Lord, who are the reapers? My holy angels
who will attend Me when the harvest of the
earth is ripe, and I come in My glory to reap
it. (Rev. 14 : 14; Matt. 25 : 31). And when,
Lord, when shall the harvest be? The harvest is the end of the world. The end of the
world! But, most gracious Master, can this
be so? Are these pernicious tares—is all this
tangled mass of confusion and evil which they
represent to continue until then? Must not
the latter day of glory shine upon this now
wretched earth before Thy second coming—
that day when all things that offend shall be
cast out of Thy kingdom, and Thy people
shall be all righteous, and the righteous shall
shine forth as the sun? No; replies the
Master, let both grow together; the wicked
with the godly; shameless hypocrites with
true saints; those who do iniquity with those
who follow the Lamb, until the harvest; until
the end of the world; until the Son of Man

shall come with the clouds of heaven for judgment. " Pregnant words," as Trench well says,
"which tell us that evil is not, as so many
dream, gradually to wane and disappear before
the good, and the world to find itself in the
Church ; but, each to unfold itself more fully
out of its own root, after its own kind, till, at
last they stand face to face, each in its highest
manifestation in the persons of Christ and
Anti-Christ ; on the one hand, an incarnate
God ; or the other, the man in whom the fulness of all Satanic power will dwell bodily.
Both are to grow until the harvest; till they
are ripe, one for destruction, and the other for
full salvation."

THE NOBLEMAN AND HIS KINGDOM.

(Luke 19 : 11–27.)

In full harmony with this is that parable of
a certain nobleman who went into a far
country to receive for Himself a kingdom and
to return. The Lord spoke it apparently
when in the house of Zaccheus. It was on

the week before His death.   As on His
journey, He drew nigh to Jerusalem, some of
those who were with Him, thought the kingdom of God would immediately appear.   Who
could tell but when He reached the royal city,
He would proclaim Himself the Messiah, the
mighty King?   It was a grave error.   Unless
dissipated it would work evil.   Many most
essential and wonderful things must take place
before His coronation day.   In this parable,
therefore, He shadowed forth the real truth.
By the nobleman, He means Himself.   By
the going into a far country to receive a kingdom, He means His own going up to the
throne of the Father, who has promised Him
the kingdom, and in due time will invest Him
with it.   By the conduct of His servants and
His citizens, He means to set forth what men
in this world will be and do during His
absence.   By the return, He means His own
second coming.

Our Lord, then, has gone away to receive
for Himself a kingdom.   Centuries have since

passed, and He is still absent. The implication is that He has not yet received that for which He went; *i. e.*, that special kingdom, which the parable contemplates, for, upon receiving it, He was to return. And this implication is made sure by the clear foreshowing of the prophet. (Dan. 7: 13, 14). It is true, indeed, that the divine Son received this kingdom by promise, in the eternal covenant. It is also true that He made perfect His indefeasible right to it, when, having become incarnate, He offered Himself without spot unto God on Calvary. But it is equally plain that His formal and visible investiture with it is still in the future. The Messianic kingdom—that special dominion, which, as the God-Man Redeemer He will exercise upon His own throne, in distinction from that which He now exercises upon His Father's throne, is to be given to Him by the Ancient of days, when He shall come with the clouds of heaven. This kingdom is an everlasting one; and under it, all people, nations and languages shall serve Him.

Besides which, observe this further truth set forth in the parable. The return of the Lord, having received the kingdom, is His second coming. His absence, therefore, is to extend from His ascension to heaven from the Mount of Olives in the sight of wondering witnesses, to His descent from heaven, with the voice of the archangel, and with the trumpet of God. Now, what will be the spiritual aspects of the intervening period? Christ himself has told us in the parable. He bade His servants, "Occupy till I come!" These servants represent the visible Church. Some of them are faithful and will receive their reward. Others of them prove unfaithful. They betray their holy trust, and seek to vindicate themselves by impeaching the Master. How the facts, so far, correspond with the prediction. But, He also has His citizens. These represent the world outside of the Church. The parable shows them in positive rebellion. They hate Him. They send a message after Him. They cry out, we will not have this man to reign

9

over us. Could there be a truer representa-
tion of the feelings and course of the mass of
men towards their absent, but rightful Lord
and King?   It has been so along the past,
since He went away.   It is so now, among the
most civilized, as well as among the most bar-
barous. What throngs of unfaithful servants
in the Church ! What bitter and pronounced
opposition to Christ through the nations!
The world over, individual sentiment, social
customs, public laws, the dominant spirit and
action of the race cry out aloud, " We will not
have this man to reign over us!" According
to the parable, this state of things will last
until the Lord shall come and take account of
His servants and His citizens.   Until then,
therefore, there can be no millennium.

PROPHECY OF THE LORD.

(Matt. 24 : 1- 51).

Having spoken this parable, the Lord went
before, ascending up to Jerusalem.   It was on
Friday, apparently, that He reached Bethany,

the home of Martha and Mary and Lazarus. The morrow would be the first day of the great week—week filled with events of infinite interest. Two days before the passover, the Saviour took His departure from the temple and the city, saying, " Behold, your house is left unto you desolate. For I say unto you, ye shall not see me henceforth till ye shall say Blessed is He that cometh in the name of the Lord." Crossing then the Cedron and going up the Mount of Olives, He sat there gazing, in sadness, on the scenes He had just left. Eager for fuller knowledge of those amazing events which He so often had intimated would come, His disciples gather around Him and ask, " When shall these things be ? And what shall be the sign of Thy coming, and of the end of the world?" The time and the circumstances rendered the inquiry a most fitting one, and its answer a necessity, not only for their fuller knowledge, but also for their support in the dread experience they were so soon to have as His disciples. He, therefore opened His mouth and uttered that memorable discourse, which may well be called the great prophecy of the Lord himself concerning the last days, and concerning His own coming again in glory. Some of its details may perplex us. In a portion of it, too, there is, doubtless, a parallel between events connected with the destruction of the Jewish economy, and events which will be connected with the closing up of the present dispensation. But its outline and its essential meaning are clear as the sun. It reaches from the time then present, to the day of the coming of the Son of Man in the clouds of heaven with power and great glory. Look at it, then, and point out where, by any possibility it implies the millennium before that day. Look at it and point out where it does not utterly exclude the millennium before that day. It tells of wars and rumors of wars; of nations and kingdoms in turmoil and deadly conflict; of famines, and pestilences and earthquakes. It tells of affliction and persecution in the

Church ; of false brethren, of false prophets, and false Christs having great power ; and of the large decay of love, because of abounding iniquity. It tells of the times of the Gentiles, during the whole remaining course of which Jerusalem shall be trodden down, as we see at this day. It tells of the preaching of the Gospel of the kingdom, in all the world, for a testimony unto all nations. It tells of a tribulation, unequaled for its severity, either before or after it, and which seems to be meant by the prophet Daniel, where he says, " And there shall be a time of trouble, such as never was since there was a nation, even to that same time ; and, at that time Thy people shall be delivered, every one that shall be found written in the book." (12 : 1). It tells of wide-spread religious indifference, and of absorption in the things of this life, so that, at length, it will be as it was in the days before the flood ; men, everywhere, eating and drinking, buying and selling, planting and building, marrying and giving in marriage, with almost

no spiritual care, until the great sound of the
trumpet startles them into thought and feeling.   It further declares that "immediately
after the tribulation of those days, the sun
shall be darkened and the moon shall not give
her light ; and the stars shall fall from heaven,
and the powers of heaven shall be shaken ;"
and then, in the midst of these things the Son
of Man shall come.   Such is the picture which
the divine Lord gives of the earthly panorama,
from the time of His public passion to the
time of His public crowning.   Who can see
in it the millennium ?   Where across its deep
darkness shines the wondrous glory of those
thousand years ?   Nay, where is there one
gleam of that glory, until it flashes from the
presence of the Lord himself, as He comes in
the clouds of heaven for judgment and to
reign.

THE SLEEPING VIRGINS.
(Matt. 25: 1–13).

To illustrate and impress this solemn
prophecy, the Lord immediately added the

parable of the virgins, the parable of the tal-
ents, and a most impressive description of the
judgment to come. With this His public ministry ended. The parable of the virgins sheds
a strong light on the present inquiry. Glance
at it, with this reference :

"Then shall the kingdom of heaven be
likened unto ten virgins, which took their
lamps, and went forth to meet the Bridegroom."

Then. When? While the Bridegroom is
gone. Not necessarily and only at the close of
this age, but also along its whole course, whenever the Lord's servants shall say in their
heart, The Lord delayeth His coming, and
shall therefore give freer scope to the lusts of
the flesh and the world. This unbelief may
become deeper, as the supreme hour draws
nigh, but how much has it characterized the
Church of the past. With what mournful
power does it hold and benumb the Church of
to-day !

And who are the virgins? Can there be

a doubt? Ten is the number of complete-
ness. Paul wrote of the Church in Corinth
"as a chaste virgin, espoused unto Christ."
The ten virgins, therefore, represent the
Church of the Lord among men; the visible
Church. Some of these virgins have the true
divine life in their souls, and, therefore, the
essential preparation for meeting the Bridegroom. Some of them have not this life, and,
therefore, as the result shows, have not this
preparation. They are alike called virgins,
because of their common profession; and to
the extent of this profession they are alike
espoused unto Christ. He is the Bridegroom.
But He is absent. He has gone away to
receive a kingdom. In due time He will
return. To the first disciples, it was a sad
moment when He said, I go away, even
though He added, I will come again. The
words filled them with sorrow. And when
they stood gazing upward until the cloud
received Him from their sight, their most
earnest hope was that His return would be

soon. And, when presently they found themselves, as sheep among wolves, and persecution began, and its fires became fiercer and still
more fierce, O! how they yearned for the
Lord to come. Their loins were girded, and
their lamps trimmed and burning. But the
Bridegroom delayed. Disappointment, it may
be, touched the nerve of faith. The terrible
storms around them grew less terrible. Instead of scoffs, prisons, flames, there gradually
came respect, honor, influence, even the throne
and crown of this world. By some process,
whether this or that, it was soon enough true
of the virgins that " they all slumbered and
slept." Men may question the exact degree
of the insensibility thus indicated, but it is
positive and deep, especially with reference to
the coming of the Bridegroom.

Have the virgins awaked? When will they
awake? How long will they still slumber
and sleep? How long will the Church of the
Lord remain in this strange spiritual insensibility? Turn to the parable. It answers,

while the Bridegroom tarries; up to the very moment of His appearance. They are roused only by the midnight cry, "Behold the Bridegroom cometh, go ye out to meet Him." Will you insist that the millennium must come and go before the return of the Bridegroom? Then the virgins will slumber and sleep through all that illustrious period. While those scenes surpassing fable which Isaiah and his fellow prophets so vividly depict are opening on every side, while the full beams of the latter day of glory are spreading holy beauty and gladness all around, and the mountain of the Lord's house is established in the tops of the mountains, the virgins, the Church espoused unto Christ, will be sunk in this deep spiritual insensibility! Is this simply and absolutely impossible? Then there can be no millennium before the Bridegroom comes.

TIMES OF RESTITUTION.
(Acts 3: 19–21).

The Lamb of God has now been offered. The resurrection has taken place, and He who died has thus been declared to be the Son of God with power. He has ascended on high, leading captivity captive, and given gifts to men. He has sent down upon His servants the Holy Ghost, in the extraordinary manifestations of the day of Pentecost, and in that permanent presence, in which He will abide with the Church until the Lord himself shall return. Peter is preaching his second recorded sermon. Deeply moved by the healing of the lame man at the gate Beautiful of the temple, the people are crowding around the two apostles in Solomon's porch. He disclaims for himself and John the merit of that mighty work, and the power by which it was wrought. He tells them that Jesus was the Healer; that Jesus is the Prince of Life, the Holy One and the Just; and that in Him alone is salvation. "Repent, therefore, He cries, Oh! ye men of Israel, and be converted for the blotting out of your sins; so that the times of refreshing shall come from the presence of the Lord, and He shall send Jesus Christ, which before was preached unto you ; whom the heaven must receive, until the times of restitution of all things, which God hath spoken by the mouth of all His holy prophets since the world began." As the discourse moves thus earnestly and grandly on, the apostles are put under sudden arrest, and spend the night in prison.

Examine these words. They present a cluster of great thoughts, every one of which merits the most careful attention.

1. By the same Spirit who dwelt in the prophets, Peter renews the prophecy of " the times of refreshing." They had not been realized in the history of the Church up to his day. He means those signal times of spiritual triumph, rest and joy, which Christian faith and hope look forward to as the millenium.

2. As Paul affirms that the destruction of the wicked will issue " from the presence of the Lord, when He shall come to be glorified in His saints," so Peter also teaches that " the times of refreshing " will come—whatever may be true of creature agencies and powers—

"from the presence of the Lord," at the same coming.

3. He also teaches that the coming of these times of refreshing depends, in some sense and degree, on the repentance and conversion of the Jewish people ; for the true and only defensible rendering of his words is, "Repent ye, therefore, and be converted unto the blotting out of your sins, so that, or in order that, the times of refreshing may come." Paul, doubtless, referred to the same thing when he wrote, "Through their fall salvation is come to the Gentiles. But then, if the casting away of them be the reconciling of the world, what shall the receiving of them be but life from the dead ?"

4. The apostle, moreover, connects "the times of refreshing," chronologically, with the sending of Jesus Christ, whom the heaven has received. This sending of Jesus Christ cannot be the first sending. That had already occurred when Peter thus spoke. The Lord had both come and gone. Peter had seen

Him and lived with Him. He had heard Him, and believed on Him. His own eyes had followed Him as He went up into heaven whence He came. This sending, therefore, must be the coming in glory.

5. When will this coming in glory be? Peter gives a most certain answer when he says, " Whom the heaven must receive, until the times of restitution of all things, which God hath spoken by the mouth of all His holy prophets." How explicit and conclusive! "The times of restitution " and " the times of re- freshing " are not only contemporaneous ; they also coalesce. The differing forms of ex- pression point at differing aspects of the same times. " The times of restitution " include "the times of refreshing." " The times of re- freshing " flow from and are a part of " the times of restitution." They are now prophecy. They will become history, in that great period currently called the millennium. Peter, there- fore, really says, that Jesus Christ is to remain

where He now is—in the heaven—on the
throne of the Father, until the millennium.
There can, therefore, be no millennium before
the Lord shall come. Some, indeed, who
spiritualize, as it is called, these apostolic statements, insist that until the times of restitution
means during those times. This, however, is
not the natural and obvious meaning of the
word until. It can be gained in this place
only by pressure. Besides which, it does not
meet the want of those who thus press it.
Their theory is that the second coming of the
Lord cannot occur until after the millennium.
But if they will say that Peter here means by,
until the millennium, until after it, they do not
interpret the word of God; they wrest it ; and
they wrest this particular Scripture out of perfect harmony with every other Scripture which
directly touches the time of the Lord's coming. The heaven whither the Lord has gone,
will retain Him until " the times of restitution."
He will then come again ; and inaugurating

those times, He will fill them with the bene-
dictions and all the glories of His kingly
presence and power.

THE GREAT APOSTASY.

(2 Thess. 2: 1–12).

It is possible that Saul of Tarsus heard this
preaching of Simon Peter, in Solomon's porch.
It is probable that he was present in the Coun-
cil, when Stephen, with words of the Holy
Ghost, cut to their heart those who heard him.
It is certain that he saw and took part in the
stoning and death of the first martyr. Presently, however, he also bows down in penitence, in faith, in adoring love before Jesus
Christ.   From that moment his life is a conse-
cration. Damascus, Arabia, Jerusalem, An
tioch, Cyprus, the whole of accessible Asia
hear him proclaiming Jesus Christ as the One
Saviour of lost men. At the bidding of the
Spirit, he then crosses the Ægean Sea into
Europe, and there lifts up the banner, and
tells and tells again the wondrous story of the

cross.   At Philippi they beat him with many
stripes, and cast him, covered with blood, into
prison, but he gathers a Church of Christ.
Released, he goes thence to Thessalonica,
and there again from souls that were dead
raises a living body of them that believe.   To
this Church he sends his first apostolic letters ;
the first of those which were to be a permanent part of the divine revelation.   In one of
these letters he puts on record a most notable
prophecy.   There will be, he says, within the
Church of Christ, an apostasy, the apostasy.
This apostasy will at length head up in the
man of sin, the son of perdition.   It will begin
unobserved.   It will advance gradually.   It
will become most unrighteous and deceiving.
It will gain Satanic craft, power and success.
The apostle had, indeed, already preached this
to the Thessalonians before thus writing it.
" Remember ye not, that when I was yet with
you, I told you these things ? "   He recurred
to it now, to arrest and crush out an error
just rising in the Church.   Somehow the

10

Christians in Thessalonica conceived that the day of Christ had come; that its beginning was actually upon them. Not so; said Paul. The apostasy of which I have told you, must first come, and the man of sin be revealed. Meantime, the Lord will remain in the heaven which received Him.

The apostasy! A falling away in the Church of our Lord! When, thou man of God, will this be? The Spirit had not made known the time of its manifestation. Paul, therefore, could not declare it. He only said, "The mystery of iniquity doth already work." The seeds of the terrible evil are even now planted. The secret leaven is diffusing itself. But at present there is a restraining power. When this power shall be taken away the apostasy will begin to be manifest. The restraining power was the power of pagan Rome. So all the Fathers believed, and rightly. When this power gave way to nominally Christian Rome, the development of the evil, which had been repressed, was visible and rapid. The spirit of the world in the Church, secularity, ambition, corruption ran riot, and all too soon the man of sin sat enthroned in the temple of God. There have been and are other apostasies in the visible Church, but the history of this apostasy is the history of Papal Rome.

How long is this apostasy to last? What period in the life of the Church and the world is it destined to cover? When will its mighty and malignant power end? Listen: "Whom the Lord Jesus shall consume with the spirit of His mouth, and destroy with the brightness of His coming." What coming? There can be but one answer — His second coming. The destruction of the man of sin is to come from the personal presence of the Lord. That presence will be as a consuming fire. Chrysostom said: "As fire in its progress consumes little insects by its heat before it touches them, so the mere approach of Christ will be enough to consume Anti-Christ." Nothing, however, but this will do it. He

will still sit in the temple of God, making his
impious pretensions, and exercising his baleful
influence, until the brightness of the coming
of the Lord shall destroy him.   Then only
will sound forth that exulting cry: "Rejoice
over her, thou heaven, and ye saints and
apostles and prophets, for God hath avenged
you on her!" (Rev. 18: 20.)   Until then,
therefore, there can be no millennium.

THE FIRST RESURRECTION.
(Rev. 20: 4–6.)

To these testimonies of Peter and Paul, the
beloved John adds that which was made
known to him on Patmos.   There, when in
the Spirit, on the Lord's day, he saw Satan
bound and shut up for a thousand years—*i. e.*,
during the millennium.   Immediately upon
this suppression of Satan, he saw those who
had died in Christ, and as true witnesses for
Christ, living and reigning with Him through
the same thousand years, or through the millennium.   He also saw that the rest of the

dead—*i. e.,* those who were not dead in Christ
—did not then live again, but remained in
their graves until the millennium was past.
This living again, and exaltation of the holy
dead, at the beginning of the thousand years
or the millennium, he designates as the first
resurrection.

Surely this record of John would seem to
be plain and decisive. It is a record of literal
facts, although it is made in figurative language.
Lest, however, because of the figures, the
meaning of the Spirit might not be clearly
seen, there is added an explanation. Just as
in the first chapter of the book, the seven
stars and the seven candlesticks are symbols,
and the Spirit explains them thus :—The seven
candlesticks are the seven Churches, and the
seven stars are the seven angels or pastors of
the Churches—so here, the living again and
enthronement of those who are Christ's, when
the millennium begins, is explained to be the
first resurrection. Of course, this resurrection
is wrought by Christ. No voice but His can

penetrate the graves and quicken the dead. As, therefore, this resurrection takes place before the millennium, or at its opening, so the second coming of Christ must take place then, inasmuch as, according to Holy Scripture, this coming is to be gloriously signalized by this resurrection.

But, is not this doctrine of the first resurrection a new doctrine? What if it were so? God has now, at least, clearly revealed it. It is, therefore, true. All divine revelation has been gradual, from less to more. Each doctrine in this revelation, has been put there, at first, in its seed form. The growth of the doctrine has corresponded to the progress of the revelation.

This, however, is not a new doctrine in either the history of the Church or in the revelations of the eternal Spirit. Almost the whole body of the saints in the New Testament period and in the period immediately succeeding, believed in, and rejoiced in view of, the first resurrection. How far this faith may have rested on the oral teaching of inspired men we do not know; but it also had an ample ground in that which is written. Note some of the data :

1. There will be a resurrection of the dead ; and of all the dead. This the whole Church believes, and has believed from the beginning, for so the Holy One most clearly reveals.

2. Whenever, in the Scriptures, the resurrections of the righteous and the wicked come into view together, that of the righteous dead invariably has the precedence in the order of mention.

3. In illustrating and commending that beneficence which seeks, and which has, no recompense from men, the Saviour said : — " Thou shalt be blessed, for thou shalt be recompensed at the resurrection of the just." There is to be then " the resurrection of the just." It implies as its contrast a resurrection of the unjust. (Luke 14 : 14).

4. Observe also, this : " The children of this world," said the Saviour, " marry and are given

in marriage.   But, they which shall be accounted worthy to obtain that world "—*i. e.,* the
next age or dispensation—" and the resurrection from the dead, neither marry nor are given
in marriage." (Luke 20: 35).   What almost
novel ideas to us, who so carelessly read, even
Holy Scripture.   Note them.   There is, indeed,
to be a resurrection of all the dead, irrespect-
ive of moral character and desert.   Here,
however, a class of men is brought into view,
who, in distinction from the children of this
world, will be deemed worthy to obtain the
resurrection.   What resurrection ?   Not merely
the resurrection of the dead.   The words of
the Saviour here are definite; they say, the
resurrection which is out of, or, from among
the dead.   It is that resurrection which will
still leave some of the dead in their graves.   It
is plainly, therefore, a first resurrection.

5. Again.   In his most interesting presenta-
tion of this subject, in 1 Cor. 15 : 1–58, the
apostle Paul re-affirms the resurrection of the
dead, and of all the dead.   He also makes

some very clear distinctions with reference to it. There is an appointed order. Every one will be raised in his own class or company. Christ is already risen as " the first fruits of them that slept." Those who are dead in Christ will be raised in their order when Christ shall come. The apostle does not definitely say when the rest of the dead will be raised in their order, but his statements irresistibly imply that it will not be then—*i. e.*, when the dead in Christ arise. It will be after that. The resurrection of the saints, therefore, at Christ's coming relative to that of the rest of the dead who are not raised then, is a first resurrection.

6. In his beautiful letter to the church at Philippi, the first fruit of his evangelical labor in Europe, Paul expresses a most sincere desire with reference to his own personal resurrection. Above everything else he wants to know Christ; he wants to win Christ; he wants to be found in Christ and to be clothed with His righteousness. He wants also to

know the power of Christ's resurrection and
the fellowship of Christ's sufferings, and to be
made conformable to Christ's death, " if, by
any means," he adds, " I might attain unto the
resurrection of the dead." His whole soul is
on fire with reference to this momentous
result.

What now is Paul's meaning? He is per-
fectly sure of a resurrection. Whether he
knows Christ or not, he will certainly, at some
time, come up out of the grave. Why, then,
this so vehement desire? What does he so
yearningly want? Not, a resurrection, but
the resurrection. Nor does he merely want
the resurrection of the dead. This rendering
does not express the heart of Paul or the
mind of the Spirit. The words here are like
the words, just noted, which the Saviour used
of those who shall be accounted worthy of the
age or dispensation to come. Paul's irrepres-
sible longing was for that resurrection which
shall be out of, or, from among the dead; that
resurrection which will leave some of the

dead not raised; the resurrection of the just; the resurrection unto life; the resurrection of those who are Christ's at His coming ; in a word, the first resurrection.

We return thus to the testimony of John. It is given in figure. It is therefore new as to form. In this form, however, it sets forth precisely the same facts, which, in literal terms, are attested by the apostle Paul, and by the divine Lord Himself. The living again of the saintly dead, before the millennium, is the first resurrection. They are raised then from among the dead. The rest of the dead do not live again until the millennium is past. The first resurrection will be wrought by Christ at His coming. His coming, therefore, must precede the millennium. And so the continuous voice of Holy Scripture bids us look for the latter day of glory, only when the King of glory shall come in befitting array to execute judgment in the earth, and to sit upon the throne of His glory.

THE THRONE OF HIS GLORY.
(Matt. 19: 26; 25: 31).

The throne of His glory. What a contrast this will be to the cross of His shame! But He foresaw it and foretold it. It was a part of the joy set before Him. When, therefore, He was entering into the darkness and death of the cross, He lifted up His voice and spoke to the disciples of His glorious throne. "When the Son of Man," He said, "shall come in His glory, and all the holy angels with Him, then shall He sit upon the throne of His glory." So a few days earlier when Peter asked Him, "What therefore shall we have who have forsaken all and followed Thee?" "Jesus said unto them, Verily I say unto you, that in the Palingenesia"—the times of restitution, the millennial times—"when the Son of Man shall sit upon the throne of His glory, ye also shall sit on twelve thrones, judging the twelve tribes of Israel."

There can be no doubt that the coming of the Son of Man in His glory, and all the holy angels with Him, is His second coming. At that coming, therefore, He will sit upon the throne of His glory. And, as we shall see, He will not sit upon the throne of His glory until then. The Palingenesia, therefore, cannot have its realization before the Lord shall come; for in the Palingenesia He will sit upon the throne of His glory; or His glorious throne. His throne, not the throne of another. His throne as the Son and heir of David; His throne as the triumphant Messiah; His throne as the God-Man Redeemer ruling over His redeemed; that throne, of which the immutable Word says, it shall endure forever and ever.

But is not Christ now upon His throne? Many so affirm, because by the spiritualizing process they obliterate clear and divine distinctions, but the Scriptures answer, No; Christ is now upon the Father's throne. Hear the voice of the witnesses: In foresight of the Messiah's exaltation the Psalmist wrote, " The Lord said unto my Lord, sit thou at my right hand." It was the voice of Jehovah the Father to David's Lord, or the Messiah. (Matt. 22 : 41–46). He shall sit there how long? Forever? No. "Sit Thou at my right hand until I make thine enemies thy footstool." (Ps. 110: 1). The Messiah, therefore, or the risen and ascended Christ was to sit at the right hand of God the Father; or upon the Father's throne. His sitting there, however, was not to be permanent. It was for a definite purpose, and a limited and specified time. It would end when the enemies of the Messiah should be subdued. This most explicit voice of the Spirit is renewed and prolonged in the New Testament. Jesus said to the Sanhedrim, " Hereafter ye shall see the Son of Man sitting on the right hand of power." (Matt. 26 : 64). The evangelist Mark said, "So then, after the Lord had spoken unto them, He was received up into heaven, and sat on the right hand of God." (Mark 16 : 20). Stephen the first martyr said, " Behold I see the heavens opened and the Son of Man standing on the right hand of God." (Acts 7: 36). The apostle Paul said, " He raised Him from the dead, and set Him at His own right hand." " Who is even at the right hand of God." " Seek those things which are above where Christ sitteth on the right hand of God." " This man, after He had offered one sacrifice for sins forever, sat down on the right hand of God." " Who, for the joy that was set before Him, endured the cross, despising the shame, and is set down on the right hand of the throne of God." (Eph. 1 : 20; Rom. 8 : 30; Col. 3 : 1 ; Heb. 10 : 12 ; 12 : 2). The apostle Peter also said, ' Who is gone into heaven, and is on the right hand of God." (1 Pet. 3 : 22). Such is the concord of the gospels and the epistles. They alike tell us that Jesus Christ is at the right hand of God, or on the throne of God; and that He will remain there, (1 Cor. 15 : 24 ; Heb. 10 : 13,) just as the Psalmist foretold, until His enemies are made His footstool. To be on the throne of God is to have and to exercise the authority and power which pertain to that throne. But more than this. The first Christian century runs its course. It is seventy years almost since the risen Christ ascended. The heavens open and the voice of the Lord himself comes resounding thence : "To him that overcometh, will I grant to sit with Me in My throne, even as I also overcame and am set down with the Father in His throne;" words which ought to have been the battle-cry of the Church along the ages.

Mark them. The Son of Man, the Messiah overcame. Who can express or concieve the greatness either of His conflict or His victory, He is therefore set down ; not upon His own throne, but with the Father in His throne. What does this mean ? What can it mean, except that He is now invested with, and exercises the authority and power which belong to, that throne—the throne of the Father—the throne of the Godhead. In what character and relation is Christ thus enthroned ? Not as the only begotten and almighty Son, co-essential and co-eternal with the Father and the Spirit, for in this view His session there must be eternal. He sits in the Father's throne as He who, in the flesh, fought with the God of this world and all his confederate hosts and overcame them. It is therefore as the Christ, the God-Man Redeemer ; a dominion therefore which He has, not of essential right, but of most divine gift. "All power," He himself said, just as He went up on high, "is given unto Me in heaven and in earth." The power thus given He now exercises from the throne of the Father over the Church and over the worlds; over the worlds with reference to the Church. At the appointed time, this dominion of Christ will end. It is so written. His dominion as the Son of God, equal with the Father and the Spirit in being and in power and glory, will never end. In the nature of the case it is impossible. His dominion also as the Son of Man, the incarnate word, the conquering and exalted Messiah will be everlasting. This is affirmed over and over again

11

by the revealing Spirit. But this intermediate dominion, which as the Christ He now exercises upon the throne of Godhead, will close when the end for which it exists shall be accomplished. It will be delivered to God, even the Father. The Son of Man will then sit upon His own throne; the throne of His glory. This will be as He told us, at His second coming. His saints, moreover, will reign with Him. Having overcome they will then sit with Him in His throne; as He, having overcome, now sits with the Father in His throne. Many times the Scriptures sound out this vast promise. They love to repeat it. When Christ thus sits upon the throne of His glory, the Palingenesia will have come, the regeneration—the times of restitution and refreshing from the presence of the Lord— the latter day of the glory of the Church and her mighty King upon the earth.

What Christ-loving soul will not, with Milton, cry aloud, "Come forth out of thy royal chambers, O Prince of the Kings of the earth.

Put on the visible robes of thy imperial majesty. Take up that unlimited sceptre which thy almighty Father hath given thee; for now the voice of thy Bride calls thee; and all creatures sigh to be renewed?" And also with the beloved John, as in the Spirit he closes the great revelation on Patmos, " Come, Lord Jesus, come quickly ! "

> " Come, blessed Lord, bid every shore
>   And answering island sing
> The praises of Thy royal name,
>   And own Thee as their King.
>
> Bid the whole earth, responsive now
>   To the bright world above,
> Break forth in rapturous strains of joy,
>   In memory of Thy love.
>
> Lord, Lord, Thy fair creation groans,
>   The air, the earth, the sea,
> In unison with all our hearts,
>   And calls aloud for Thee.
>
> Thine was the cross, with all its fruits,
>   Of grace and peace divine;
> Be thine the crown of glory now,
>   The palm of victory thine."

POWER AND USE OF THIS
HOPE.

POWER AND USE OF THIS HOPE.

" Every man that hath this hope in Him, purifieth himself, even as He is pure." (1 John 3 : 3).

" Till the day dawn,
And the Day-star arise,
 Church of the Living God,
 Pursue thy upward road ;
 Look not behind, nor stray
 From the well-trodden way.
 Be not ashamed to bear
 Thy cross on earth, nor fear
 Reproach and poverty
 For Him who died for thee.
 With girded loins press on,
 Till the reward is won ;
 Think of thy absent Lord,
 Hold fast thy plighted word.
Doff not the weeds of widowhood, nor fear
To let the world, through which thou passest, hear
The widow's cry, and see the widow's faithful tear."

TRUTH is to the soul what food is to the body. As the law, therefore, those must grow in knowledge who would grow in grace.

Each particular truth has its own fitness and power with reference to the spiritual life ; but all truth in due combination is necessary in order to "the measure of the stature of the fulness of Christ;" and that "the man of God may be perfect, thoroughly furnished unto to all good works."

The Scriptures, however, give prominence to some truths. They repeat them and emphasize them as of special moment. What is the essential story of the Gospel? It is Immanuel—God with us on the cross and in the grave; the life and hope of the world. Without this there would be no Gospel. But suppose the Gospel had left Immanuel on the cross, or in the grave. Then were our preaching vain, and your faith also vain. Christ risen again is indispensable to any saving power of Christ crucified. Christ at the right hand of God is as essential as Christ slain by the hands of wicked men. His coming in weakness and sorrow has its purposed and true end in His coming again in power and in great glory.

ITS PLACE IN THE BIBLE.

Look at the place of this truth in the Bible. The preceding pages have shown how the second coming of the Lord enters into the substance of the Old Testament, and was the faith and hope of the prophets. They have also shown how the light of that coming pours itself over all the New Testament; and was the faith and hope of the evanglists and apostles. The Saviour himself often spoke of His coming glory, and on the Mount of Transfiguration gave some anticipatory gleams of it. In almost His last words in the Gospels, He said, " I will come again and receive you unto Myself; that where I am, there ye may be also." The Acts open with the testimony of the angels. Scarcely had the cloud received the ascending Lord from human sight, when they said, " This same Jesus which is taken up from you into heaven shall so come in like manner, as ye have seen Him go into heaven." A few days later, and while Pentecostal wonders were all around them, Peter and John are looking forward and telling of "the times of refreshing from the presence of the Lord," and of "the times of restitution of all things" in the future. In all the epistles, except that to Philemon, and those brief sentences, composing the second and third epistles of John, the coming of the Lord has a frequent place, and this not merely as a fact, but as a fact of most signal moment, and as meant to exert a mighty moral power. In the first two letters of Paul, those to the Thessalonians, every chapter rings with the blessed sound. In the last two letters of the same apostle the same heavenly music is still heard. Listen, as he says to Titus:

" The grace of God that bringeth salvation hath appeared unto all men, teaching us that denying ungodliness and worldly lusts, we should live soberly, righteously, and godly in this present world ; looking for that blessed hope, the glorious appearing of the great God and our Saviour Jesus Christ."

Hear him also, as standing at the very point where the two worlds meet, he thus pleads with Timothy :

" Watch thou in all things ; endure afflictions ; do the work of an evangelist ; make full proof of thy ministry, for I am now ready to be offered, and the time of my departure is at hand. I have fought a good fight; I have finished my course ; I have kept the faith ; henceforth there is laid up for me a crown of righteousness, which the Lord the righteous Judge shall give me at that day ; and not to me only, but unto all them also that love His appearing." And when we come to the Apocalypse, what is it from beginning to end but the revelation of Jesus Christ in His glory. Such is the teaching on this point of the goodly fellowship of the prophets, and of the glorious company of the apostles. For the first three centuries the Church cherished it,

and the quality and power of her faith and
hope were attested by the blood of her noble
army of martyrs.

Now this incorporation in the Scriptures of
the glorious coming of the Lord ; this causing
the light of it to brighten the whole record
from the paradise lost to the paradise restored,
was not an arbitrary thing. It was not as a
mere embellishment. It was not for a class
of Christian men and women whose taste or
culture might be pleased by this so glowing
imagery of the Spirit, as they would be by
the fancies and decorations of a great poem.
It was because it was essential to the com-
pleteness of the divine word, and to the highest life and blessing of the redeemed Church.
It was for the same great end for which all
supernatural revelation has been made, and
the whole ministry of that revelation has been
given ; " for the perfecting of the saints ; for
the edifying of the body of Christ till we all
come in the unity of the faith and of the
knowledge of the Son of God, unto a perfect

man ;" that the individual Christian and the collective Church may be fully prepared for work and conflict, for suffering and triumph.

SPECIFICATIONS.

Pass on from this general view. Beyond question, the Bible teaches the great doctrine of the glorious coming of the Lord.   This doctrine, therefore, must enter as an essential power into the building up of the Christian character and life. But, how do the Scriptures use it ?   How do they bring it from the abstract into the concrete, from doctrine into practice ?   What applications do they make of it to the every-day needs of men in this world ?   In what manner does the Holy Ghost press upon the Bride those glorious certainties connected with the return of the Bridegroom so that they may clothe the present with their own beauty, sacredness and power ?   Take some specimens.

THE SCOFFERS.

(2 Tim. 3: 1–8 ; 2 Pet. 3 : 3–10).

The Holy One, first of all, arraigns and rebukes the men who scoff at the Lord's coming. There will be such men. In the last days, is the testimony, perilous times shall come. Men will be lovers of pleasure more than lovers of God. Having the form of godliness they will deny its power. They will resist the truth. They will become reprobate concerning the faith. They will walk in their own lusts. Unbelief will keep pace with impiety. Impiety will, sooner or later, show itself in scoffing. When faithful ones here and there utter the admonitions of truth, the shout will go up, " Aha ! where, where is the promise of His coming ? The heavens above us are now just as they were at the beginning ! This firm earth will never be moved ! Away with your idle tales !" Perhaps the perilous times have already come. Certainly there are scoffers even now. But, whether now or then, what shall we do? Listen: " I charge thee before God, and the Lord Jesus Christ, who shall judge the quick and the dead at His appearing and His kingdom—preach the Word." " The day of the Lord will come as a thief in the night; in the which the heavens will pass away with a great noise, and the elements shall melt with fervent heat; the earth also, and the works that are therein, shall be burned up."

SLOTHFUL SERVANTS.
(Matt. 24: 48; Luke 21 : 34).

The scoffers may be in the visible Church. Without doubt, this is the position of the slothful servants. They profess to be servants. To this extent, therefore, they own the absent Lord. They have, however, lost faith in Him. They have let go His word. He said : "I will come again ;" " Behold I will come quickly !" They say, " We see no signs." The world is moving grandly onward. Its manufactures, its commerce, its arts, its wealth, its learning, its whole sum of civilization, how imposing! Can all this be suddenly arrested? The Lord delayeth His coming. Indeed, will He ever come? Their sense of duty grows weak. Their attachments to this world grow strong. They begin to smite their fellow-servants, and to eat and drink with the drunken. Are there now any slothful servants? Do they press those around them with their own paralyzing unbelief? What then? Can the unbelief of men change the truth of God? Will not the Lord return, and return suddenly? Ought not the faithful servants to proclaim the great fact everywhere, if so be, men may be ready for His coming? Hear the voice of the Master! "The Lord of that servant shall come in a day when he looketh not for Him, and in an hour that he is not aware of, and shall cut him asunder, and appoint him his portion with the hypocrites." "Watch ye, therefore, and pray always, that ye may be accounted worthy to escape all these things that shall come to pass, and to stand before the Son of Man."

SECULAR LIFE.

(1 Cor. 6 : 1–4).

The Church is in the world, though she is not of it. The relations of each to the other, in the persons and interests which pertain to each, are most intimate. In this imperfect state, there are rights to be protected ; there are wrongs to be redressed. Sometimes questions of law and equity spring up among those for whom Christ died, and Christian brother arraigns Christian brother before un-believers. Those who sit together at the table of the Lord contend in worldly courts. Is this a seemly sight ? Can it be pleasing to the divine Master ? Must it not bring damage upon His cause and dishonor upon His name ? Ought not the differences of Christian breth-ren to be adjusted in the spirit of Christ, among themselves ? So thought the blessed

Paul. The contests in his day of Christians
with Christians before earthly tribunals, grieved
him, and called from him an earnest remons-
trance. They have not been limited to the
time of Paul, or to the Christians in Corinth.
Look now upon the Church of the Living
God. What can be done? How shall these
unsightly conflicts of believers before unbe-
lievers be made to cease? What special
argument does the Holy Ghost use for their
suppression? Turn to the record. " Dare
any of you, having a matter against another,
go to law before the unjust and not before
the saints?" Why not dare to do it? Why
not continue to do it? Why? "Do ye not
know that the saints shall judge the world?"
Will you reverse this, and have the world
judge the saints? And further, "Do ye not
know that we shall judge angels?" Shall we
then seek to be judged by sinful men? O
Church of the Lord, abase not thyself! When
the Lord comes, we shall judge the world and
the angels. We shall partake of His glory.

We shall sit with Him in His throne. He will give us power over the nations. He will make us priests and kings unto God, and we shall reign on the earth.

OFFICIAL POSITION.
(1 Pet. 5: 1–4).

When the Lord Jesus ascended up on high, He was still mindful of His Church. He sent upon it the Holy Ghost. He carried forward, within it, the divine revelation. He gave to it apostles, prophets and evangelists, for the special needs of the time then present. As the permanent gifts of His grace, He also bestowed pastors and teachers. Christ himself is the chief Shepherd of the Church. The pastors and teachers are shepherds under Christ. They have the present care of His beautiful flock. It is theirs to open to them the green pastures and refresh them from the pure waters; to gather the lambs in their arms and carry them in their bosom; to guard them against danger and evil, and present them at length faultless in the presence of

His glory. What an office and work; how high and sacred! But its possibilities of evil are equal to its possibilities for good. We have this treasure in earthen vessels. The shepherds may prove faithless and false; they may lose sight of the Master, and set at naught His most holy will; they may become hirelings, whose own the sheep are not; they may flee when they see the wolf coming; they may break down the bars of the fold and let in all manner of ravenous beasts. What sad records there are of the apostasy, the corruption, the oppression of the shepherds. The Scriptures foresaw this. They gave warning against it. They presented facts and motives for unyielding fidelity. What special fact and motive does the ever-blessed Spirit press upon the shepherds, that they may be faithful and true and holy? Simon Peter had seen the Lord in His fearful passion in the Garden, and on Calvary. He had also seen Him robed, as with the brightness of the sun, in those fore-gleams of the coming glory, on the Mount of Transfiguration. Through him, therefore, the Spirit cries with a loud voice to the shepherds, " Feed the flock of God which is among you, taking the oversight thereof, not by constraint, but willingly; not for filthy lucre, but of a ready mind; neither as being lords over God's heritage, but being ensamples to the flock. And when the Chief Shepherd shall appear, ye shall receive a crown of glory that fadeth not away." What a soul-inflaming and soul-impelling command and appeal! O ye shepherds of the flock, forget not that appearing. With most sacred vehemence covet that glorious crown.

CHRISTIAN LABOR.

(1 Cor. 15: 58).

It is the nature of life to be active, to increase and gain expression; whether it be life in a plant or life in a soul. Death alone is fixed. True religion is life. So the Scriptures constantly represent. They assume, therefore, that it will grow; that it will be-

come an increasing power for good in the
individual, and through the individual, in the
Church and the world.   Because of their new
nature, the children of God will be co-workers
with God.   How does the Holy Spirit cherish
and enlarge this life of the soul?   By what
means, over and above its own tendency, does
He draw it, or impel it, into beneficent and
holy action?   By means of truth.   What
truth?   All truth.   But truth has its special
adaptations.   This truth will fill the soul with
penitence; that will fire it with love.   This
truth will cause the soul to bow down in
adoration before the throne; that will give it
wings, as of an angel, to fly abroad, in the
ministrations of blessing.   Would you have
an example?   Paul was slain by the Law;
he was made alive by the Gospel.   Has the
Church since seen a life of so intense Christian love, or of so grand Christian work?
What special truths were they which thus
bore him up and on?   First of all, Christ on
the cross; "Who loved me," he cries, "and

gave Himself for me." Then, Christ in His glory and the saints with Him. We have seen how he longed for that resurrection, which is to be from among the dead, when the Lord shall come. It was no transient feeling. Hear him as he pleads with the Corinthians : "Therefore, beloved brethren." Pause a moment. Whence this therefore? What gives it so tremendous power? He has been telling them of the risen Christ; then of the risen saints; then of the resurrec tion body — sown in corruption, raised in incorruption; sown in dishonor, raised in glory; sown in weakness, raised in power; sown a natural body, raised a spiritual body; then of the last trump, and the change of this mortal into immortality — all at Christ's com- ing; and then He cries, " Therefore, my beloved brethren, be ye steadfast, immovable, always abounding in the work of the Lord; forasmuch as ye know that your labor is not in vain in the Lord."

PERSONAL PURITY.

(1 John 3: 2–3).

In order to its most effective expression, the divine life must be strong within. A large stream can come only from a large fountain. Holiness is power. The more holiness the more power. God's people are called to be holy, and He is their pattern, by whom they are called. " As He which hath called you is holy, so be ye holy, in all manner of conversation ; for it is written, Be ye holy for I am holy." This is the likeness of God in His children. By this they are known as born of God. The primary cause of this likeness is the divine Spirit. Its most essential means is the revealed Word. Every word of God is in order to holiness, and tends to promote it. Tell me of Christ dying for me, and how can I live any longer in sin ! Tell me of Christ rising and reigning for me, and how must my soul be drawn upward ! This is the experience of the saints. How deeply John felt the power of the cross !

How deeply, at the same time, he felt the power of the throne! "Beloved," he cried, "now are we the sons of God." It does not seem so, but it is so. And this flows from Christ. This, however, is only the beginning. "It doth not, indeed, yet appear what we shall be; but we know that when He shall appear, we shall be like Him, for we shall see Him as He is." This also will flow from Christ; that from the virtue of His death; this from the vision of His glory. What then? "Every one that hath this hope in Him purifieth himself, even as He is pure." What a clear and solemn testimony from the last of the apostles. And observe: the power of this hope to purify the soul will be according to the desire of the soul to see and be like the glorious Lord in the great day of His appearing.

PATIENCE IN TRIAL.

(Jas. 5: 7, 8).

As it was with the Saviour, so it is with the saved — the cross before the crown. God

might, indeed, take His people to Himself at
once on their regeneration. They would then
be free from all evil, and possess and enjoy
all good. In His presence there is no more
death; neither sorrow, nor crying, nor pain;
but the light which has no shade, and the
peace and joy which have no end. This, however, is not the way of God. This is not the
law of His kingdom. In calling His sons unto
glory He calls them through suffering. Look
upon the white-robed company above —
whence came they? Look upon the sacramental host below — what labor, discipline,
conflict, and trial upon trial. In the world,
too, what spread of error; what hate of truth;
what corruption of morals and manners; what
bribing of justice; what honoring of iniquity;
what oppression of the poor; what robbery of
the widow and orphan; what frauds, perjuries,
violences, on every side; until, like the souls
under the altar, we cry, "O Lord, how
long?" All this was, indeed, before known
and before written. In view of it all, the

revealing Spirit gave many a word of counsel
and comfort. This is His voice : " Count it,
brethren, all joy when ye fall into divers
temptations; knowing that the trying of your
faith worketh patience." And this : " Tribulation worketh patience, and patience experience, and experience hope, and hope maketh
not ashamed." And, still more inspiriting,
this : " Be patient, brethren, unto the coming
of the Lord. Behold, the husbandman wait-
eth for the precious fruit of the earth, and
hath long patience for it, until he receive the
early and the latter rain. Be ye also patient;
stablish your hearts, for the coming of the
Lord draweth nigh." Thou martyr at the
stake; thou prisoner in the dungeon; thou
slave writhing under the lash; thou unrecom-
pensed toiler, working yet starving; thou
plundered widow; thou beggared orphan;
thou heart-broken wife; thou father and
mother, going with sorrow to the grave; all
ye sufferers, who, while ye suffer, cling to the
crucified, be ye patient, for the Lord is com-

ing: " Behold the Judge standeth before the door."

COMFORT IN SORROW.

(1 Thess. 4 : 13–18).

What dirges of sorrow have rolled over the earth through the centuries since the Fall, and will roll until the Judgment. Whence have they sprung? From sin. Sin gave birth to sorrow. Sin is itself sorrow in the seed. Sin, when it is finished, bringeth forth death. Death is the compacted sum of all evil. Take it here as applying to the body. What home on earth has not been darkened by the dread shadow of death? What heart on earth has not been wrung and torn by the icy hand of death? Behold, the dead are more than all the living. Behold, all the living will presently be with the dead. Make room, more room for the graves of men!

Is there any healing of this world-wide sorrow? Can the abyss of death be spanned with light? It is possible. It has been done. The

divine Revealer speaks comfortable words
concerning the saintly dead. They rest, He
says, from their labors ; they have ceased from
sin. Their bodies sleep in Jesus. Their souls
still live and rejoice with the spirits of the
just made perfect. This is, indeed, comfort.
These gracious words have quieted many a
throbbing heart. They have chased away
many a hot tear. But, do even they rise up
to the full want of them who go mourning for
their dead ? Is there not yet left a deep pain
to be reached and removed, if it may be, by
the Almighty Healer of sorrow ? What then
does He further say? What still more
definite and grand revelation does He make
that this sorrow also may be gone, and even
turned into joy ? Hear Him : " I would not
have you ignorant, brethren, concerning them
which are asleep, that ye sorrow not, even as
others which have no hope. For if ye believe
that Jesus died and rose again, even so them
also which sleep in Jesus will God bring with
Him. For this we say unto you by the word

of the Lord, that we which are alive and remain unto the coming of the Lord, shall not prevent them which are asleep. For the Lord himself shall descend from heaven with a shout, with the voice of the archangel, and with the trump of God; and the dead in Christ shall rise first; then we which are alive and remain shall be caught up together with them in the clouds to meet the Lord in the air; and so shall we ever be with the Lord. Wherefore, comfort one another with these words."

CONCLUSION.

This then is that blessed hope; the glorious coming of the Lord. It is the next great epoch of the future.

The Old Testament saints looked forward to the first coming of Christ. It was their polar star. After weary ages faith was turned into sight. Men saw the Son of God incarnate. Simeon took Him in his arms. Mary sat adoring at His feet. Peter pressed close to His side. John rested on His bosom. Paul, too, saw Him on his way to Damascus, and the sight was his salvation. Jews and Gentiles saw Him and put Him to death on the cross.

The New Testament saints look forward to the second coming of Christ. This is their polar star. Again, the ages have been long and weary, but the end cometh. The world may scoff; and the Church even may let go this holy faith; but, at the appointed time, the Church and the world will see the Lord coming in power and for righteous judgment. They will see the dead in Christ living, and sitting with Him in His throne, and then the millennial glory. This vast truth pervades and inflames the Scriptures. They declare it as a divine certainty. They make it the ground of argument. They hold it up as a most powerful motive. They use it to strengthen faith, encourage hope, promote humility, fortify patience, mitigate sorrow, incite watchfulness, impel obedience, inspire prayer, increase holiness, and awaken joy. What a great blank there would be without it in even the Word of God! What a serious subtraction there would be from those sacred resources, by which His people are made strong for the work and battle of life, and to win the conqueror's crown. What wonder that Paul calls it, moved by his own sense of its grandeur, and by the special light and power of the Holy Ghost: "That blessed hope, even the glorious appearing of the great God, and our Saviour Jesus Christ."

"O what a bright and shining world,
  This groaning earth of ours will be,
When from its throne, the Tempter hurled,
  Shall leave it all, O Lord, to Thee.

O blessed Lord, with weeping eyes,
  That blissful hour we wait to see;
While every worm or leaf that dies,
  Tells of the curse, and calls for Thee.

Come Saviour, then, o'er all below
  Shine brightly from Thy throne above;
Bid heaven and earth Thy glory show,
  And all creation feel Thy love."

H 128 82

www.ingramcontent.com/pod-product-compliance
Lightning Source LLC
Chambersburg PA
CBHW032010060726
47497CB00017B/2906